SHARPENING YOUR TOEIC® L&R TEST SKILLS:

STANDARD

Seisuke Yasunami
Richard S. Lavin

Asahi Press

音声再生アプリ「リスニング・トレーナー」を使った音声ダウンロード

朝日出版社開発のアプリ、「リスニング・トレーナー（リストレ）」を使えば、教科書の音声をスマホ、タブレットに簡単にダウンロードできます。どうぞご活用ください。

◉ アプリ【リスニング・トレーナー】の使い方

《アプリのダウンロード》

App Store または Google Play から「リスニング・トレーナー」のアプリ（無料）をダウンロード

App Storeはこちら▶

Google Playはこちら▶

《アプリの使い方》

①アプリを開き「コンテンツを追加」をタップ
②画面上部に【15700】を入力しDoneをタップ

音声ストリーミング配信 》》》

この教科書の音声は、右記ウェブサイトにて無料で配信しています。

https://text.asahipress.com/free/english/

SHARPENING YOUR TOEIC® L&R TEST SKILLS: STANDARD

Cover design: Kenichiro Oshita
Photograph: Shutterstock, iStock by getty images

はしがき

　本書は、『TOEIC® テスト：初めての一歩 Starting on the TOEIC® Test』と 『TOEIC® テスト：さらなる一歩 Next Step to the TOEIC® Test』を、近年のテスト傾向に合わせて、内容を大幅に改訂したものです。これまでに学習した内容を振り返りながら、TOEIC® L&R テスト受験のために、必要な英語力の向上を目指す学生がより効果的に学べるように構成しました。

　特徴として、収録している問題は本番の問題形式に準拠していますが、Campus Life や Eating & Drinking、Entertainment など学生の皆さんに身近な日常生活の話題から、Business や Meeting、Jobs などの将来必要とされるビジネスに関するものまで、幅広いトピックが含まれています。ただ単に TOEIC® L&R テストのために学習するだけでなく、実際のコミュニケーションを想定した問題演習ができます。

　学生の皆さんが、本書を使用して、授業前の事前学習、授業中の学習、そして授業後の事後学習に励んでいただき、皆さんの英語力向上および TOEIC® L&R テストスコアアップの助けになることを願っています。

　本書の編集・校正・出版などにご尽力いただいた小林啓也氏に対して心より御礼を申し上げます。

2022 年 10 月

安浪誠祐

Richard S. Lavin

Contents

本書の使い方

UNIT 1 CAMPUS LIFE

WARM-UP Ⓐ

Match the words with their correct definitions.

(1) academic ( )   (a) a description of a course
(2) campus ( )   (b) a monetary penalty connected to study or research
(3) department ( )   (c) a place where you can borrow books
(4) fine ( )   (d) a publication that comes out a few times a year
(5) journal ( )   (e) a second-year university student
(6) library ( )   (f) a section of a university devoted to a field of study
(7) registration ( )   (g) connected to study or research
(8) semester ( )   (h) one of two periods of study in the school year
(9) sophomore ( )   (i) the process of signing up for classes
(10) syllabus ( )   (j) the site of a university

WARM-UP Ⓑ

Have the following conversation with a partner, filling in the blanks from the box below. Then listen to the recording to check your answers and intonation.

A: How's your _____ this _____?
B: It's pretty good. I have Wednesdays _____, so I can catch up with assignments. How about you?
A: Oh, mine's terrible. I failed a few _____ last year, so I'm taking more than usual.
B: Oh, no. That doesn't sound so good. Aren't you _____ part-time this semester, then?
A: No. If I fail classes again this year, I may not _____ able to graduate in four years, so I've decided to concentrate _____ my studies.

| be | courses | free | on | semester | timetable | working |

PART 1   PHOTOGRAPHS

You will hear four short statements. Look at the picture and choose the statement that best describes what you see.

1.    Ⓐ Ⓑ Ⓒ Ⓓ

2.    Ⓐ Ⓑ Ⓒ Ⓓ

PART 2   QUESTION-RESPONSE

You will hear a question or statement and three responses. Listen carefully, and choose the response to the question or statement.

3. Mark your answer.   Ⓐ Ⓑ Ⓒ
4. Mark your answer.   Ⓐ Ⓑ Ⓒ
5. Mark your answer.   Ⓐ Ⓑ Ⓒ
6. Mark your answer.   Ⓐ Ⓑ Ⓒ

2

UNIT 1 CAMPUS LIFE   3

PART 3
SHORT CONVERSATIONS:
会話問題

短めの会話を聞き取り、内容に
即して答える力を身につけます。

LANGUAGE FOCUS:
PART 5 の文法事項の確認

PART 5 で問われる文法事項を確
認し、解答に必要な文法力を高
めます。

PART 3　SHORT CONVERSATIONS

You will hear short conversations between two or more people. Listen carefully, and select the best response to each question.

Question 7 refers to the following conversation.

7. What is the weather like?
   (A) Cold
   (B) Rainy
   (C) Snowy
   (D) Windy　　　　　　　　Ⓐ Ⓑ Ⓒ Ⓓ

Questions 8 and 9 refer to the following conversation.

8. How can students access computer facilities when teachers are using computer labs?
   (A) They can fill out a form to request that a lab be made available.
   (B) They can use any of them at any time.
   (C) They can use the labs that are not reserved for classes.
   (D) They have to wait until the classes end.　Ⓐ Ⓑ Ⓒ Ⓓ

9. Where is the Clark Library located?
   (A) It's in the center of the campus.
   (B) It's near the computer facilities.
   (C) It's very large and open every day.
   (D) The main counter offers many services.　Ⓐ Ⓑ Ⓒ Ⓓ

PART 4　SHORT TALKS

You will hear short talks given by a single speaker. Listen carefully, and select the best response to each question.

Question 10 refers to the following talk.

10. When does the speaker go swimming?
    (A) Every day
    (B) Friday
    (C) Monday
    (D) Thursday　　　　　　Ⓐ Ⓑ Ⓒ Ⓓ

Questions 11 through 12 refer to the following announcement.

11. When does the registration period end?
    (A) It depends on the semester.
    (B) On the first Monday of the semester.
    (C) On the second day of the semester
    (D) On the second Friday of the semester　Ⓐ Ⓑ Ⓒ Ⓓ

12. Why is it important to register for classes before the deadline?
    (A) Failure to register will lead to a lack of opportunities in the future.
    (B) It can be done using the facilities in the central computer labs.
    (C) It has to be done on Monday.
    (D) Students who do not register for a class will not be allowed to attend that class.　Ⓐ Ⓑ Ⓒ Ⓓ

LANGUAGE FOCUS

Verb Tenses

◎ 動詞の時制を確認しながら、次の英文を読んでみましょう。

1) Look! Here **comes** the train!
   ほら、列車が来ました。
2) I hear she's **got** a new boyfriend.
   彼女には新しい彼氏ができたらしいよ。
3) It's **been** five years since we **became** friends.
   私たちが友だちになって 5 年になる。
4) When **was** America **discovered** by Columbus?
   アメリカはいつコロンブスに発見されましたか。
5) We learned that water **boils** at 100℃.
   私たちは、水は摂氏 100 度で沸騰すると習った。
6) The Olympics and Paralympics **will be held** in Los Angeles in 2028.
   オリンピックとパラリンピックは 2028 年にロサンゼルスで開催される。
7) We'll go shopping if it **has stopped** raining by this afternoon.
   午後までに雨がやんだら、買い物に行きます。

4

UNIT 1　CAMPUS LIFE　5

PART 4
SHORT TALKS:
説明問題

アナウンスメントなどの内容を
聞き取り、内容を正確に把握す
る力を養います。

PART 5
INCOMPLETE SENTENCES:
短文穴埋め問題

空所補充の問題で問われるポイントを把握し、適切に解答を選ぶ力を身に付けます。

PART 6
TEXT COMPLETION:
長文穴埋め問題

英文の文脈を理解し、空所に適切な単語を選ぶコツを身につけます。

PART 5 INCOMPLETE SENTENCES

A word or phrase is missing in each of the sentences. Select the best answer to complete the sentence.

13. He _____ a book when his mother suddenly opened the door.
    (A) has read   (B) is reading   (C) reads   (D) was reading

14. We will have finished dinner by the time you _____ here.
    (A) did get   (B) get   (C) getting   (D) got

15. She said she _____ for Paris the following week.
    (A) leave   (B) leaves   (C) will leave   (D) would leave

16. According to the schedule, we _____ on a school trip next week.
    (A) go   (B) will be going   (C) will going   (D) would go

17. I _____ ill in bed since the day before yesterday.
    (A) am   (B) had been   (C) have been   (D) was

18. I _____ such a beautiful sunset before.
    (A) has never seen   (B) never have seen   (C) never saw   (D) never see

19. If I _____ bought the house, I would have more money now.
    (A) didn't   (B) don't   (C) hadn't   (D) haven't

20. I realized that I _____ my umbrella in his car.
    (A) have left   (B) had left   (C) leave   (D) left

21. We _____ each other for five years when we got married.
    (A) had known   (B) have known   (C) knew   (D) would know

22. I lost the eraser that I _____ the day before.
    (A) brought   (B) buy   (C) had bought   (D) have bought

23. I _____ the musical four times if I go with you tomorrow.
    (A) had seen   (B) have seen   (C) will have seen   (D) will see

PART 6 TEXT COMPLETION

Read the email that follows. A word or phrase is missing in some of the sentences. Select the best answer to complete the text.

←   ★ ↰ ⋯

From the Lending Counter, Central Library
Dear Mr. Sato (Student no.: 2201056)

This is to ____ you that an item you ____ on April 17th is now overdue. Please
     24   **25**
return it without delay. Details are shown below. Please be aware that penalties

are applicable when an item becomes 8 days overdue. These may ____ ineligibility
                                              26
to borrow further items for a period and monetary fines. Details are available at

the Central Library website.

Please reply to this email or visit the Lending Counter directly if you have any

questions about this email.

Title: Read English Better!
Author: R. McDonald
Library Code: 823.1342 R21

---

24. (A) announce   (B) ask   (C) confirm   (D) inform

25. (A) borrowed   (B) have lent   (C) rented   (D) took

26. (A) consist   (B) exclude   (C) include   (D) intrude

PART 7
READING COMPREHENSION:
1つの文書・2つの文書

長めの英文を読んで内容を理解
し、設問を的確に解答する力を養
います。

Read the email that follows. Select the best answer for each question.

> ← ★ ← ···
>
> TO: ALL UNDERGRADUATE STUDENTS
> FROM: ACADEMIC AFFAIRS DIVISION
>
> ## IMPORTANT NOTICE
>
> This is to inform you of modifications to course registration rules that have come into effect this academic year.
>
> Many language courses in the general undergraduate curriculum that have until now been open only to sophomores and above will now be open to all students, including freshmen. This change is intended to give students maximum flexibility in arranging their schedules and following their interests from their first year at college.
>
> When choosing courses to take and deciding their timetables, students are advised to check that the level of any course that they wish to take is suitable. The level of each course is marked clearly in the course syllabus, listed in the Student Handbook and also available online through the Academic Affairs Division website. Students should also make themselves familiar with any additional registration guidelines of their academic department.

27. What is the purpose of this notice?
    (A) To encourage students to refer to departmental guidelines
    (B) To modify new course registration rules for sophomores and juniors
    (C) To tell students about new rules relating to language courses
    (D) To understand the levels of undergraduate language courses

28. What is the university trying to accomplish with this change?
    (A) To arrange the students' schedules with more flexibility
    (B) To encourage freshmen to learn from sophomores and juniors
    (C) To give students more choice
    (D) To make the Student Handbook easier to understand

29. What advice regarding course levels does the Academic Affairs Division give students?
    (A) To check whether the course is listed in the Student Handbook
    (B) To decide their timetable first and then discuss course levels with their academic tutor
    (C) To match the course level to their own level
    (D) To read the division's website frequently

30. What should students do in their departments?
    (A) They should check the guidelines.
    (B) They should familiarize departmental procedures.
    (C) They should follow the additional procedures.
    (D) They should go online to check whether the guidelines are reflected on the Academic Affairs Division website.

SHARPENING YOUR TOEIC® L&R TEST SKILLS:

STANDARD

WARM-UP Ⓐ

Match the words with their correct definitions.

(1) academic ( )   (a) a description of a course

(2) campus ( )   (b) a monetary penalty connected to study or research

(3) department ( )

(4) fine ( )   (c) a place where you can borrow books

(5) journal ( )   (d) a publication that comes out a few times a year

(6) library ( )   (e) a second-year university student

(7) registration ( )   (f) a section of a university devoted to a field of study

(8) semester ( )   (g) connected to study or research

(9) sophomore ( )   (h) one of two periods of study in the school year

(10) syllabus ( )   (i) the process of signing up for classes

                                                       (j) the site of a university

WARM-UP Ⓑ

Have the following conversation with a partner, filling in the blanks from the box below. Then listen to the recording to check your answers and intonation.

A: How's your _____ this _____?

B: It's pretty good. I have Wednesdays _____, so I can catch up with assignments. How about you?

A: Oh, mine's terrible. I failed a few _____ last year, so I'm taking more than usual.

B: Oh, no. That doesn't sound so good. Aren't you _____ part-time this semester, then?

A: No. If I fail classes again this year, I may not _____ able to graduate in four years, so I've decided to concentrate _____ my studies.

| be | courses | free | on | semester | timetable | working |

You will hear four short statements. Look at the picture and choose the statement that best describes what you see.

1.
(A) (B) (C) (D)

2.
(A) (B) (C) (D)

PART 2   **QUESTION-RESPONSE**

You will hear a question or statement and three responses. Listen carefully, and choose the response to the question or statement.

3. Mark your answer.   (A) (B) (C)

4. Mark your answer.   (A) (B) (C)

5. Mark your answer.   (A) (B) (C)

6. Mark your answer.   (A) (B) (C)

You will hear short conversations between two or more people. Listen carefully, and select the best response to each question.

Question 7 refers to the following conversation.

7. What is the weather like?

    (A) Cold
    (B) Rainy
    (C) Snowy
    (D) Windy
    Ⓐ Ⓑ Ⓒ Ⓓ

Questions 8 and 9 refer to the following conversation.

8. How can students access computer facilities when teachers are using computer labs?

    (A) They can fill out a form to request that a lab be made available.
    (B) They can use any of them at any time.
    (C) They can use the labs that are not reserved for classes.
    (D) They have to wait until the classes end.
    Ⓐ Ⓑ Ⓒ Ⓓ

9. Where is the Clark Library located?

    (A) It's in the center of the campus.
    (B) It's near the computer facilities.
    (C) It's very large and open every day.
    (D) The main counter offers many services.
    Ⓐ Ⓑ Ⓒ Ⓓ

You will hear short talks given by a single speaker. Listen carefully, and select the best response to each question.

Question 10 refers to the following talk.

10. When does the speaker go swimming?

    (A) Every day
    (B) Friday
    (C) Monday
    (D) Thursday
    Ⓐ Ⓑ Ⓒ Ⓓ

Questions 11 through 12 refer to the following announcement.

11. When does the registration period end?
    (A) It depends on the semester.
    (B) On the first Monday of the semester
    (C) On the second day of the semester
    (D) On the second Friday of the semester   Ⓐ Ⓑ Ⓒ Ⓓ

12. Why is it important to register for classes before the deadline?
    (A) Failure to register will lead to a lack of opportunities in the future.
    (B) It can be done using the facilities in the central computer labs.
    (C) It has to be done on Monday.
    (D) Students who do not register for a class will not be allowed to attend that
        class.   Ⓐ Ⓑ Ⓒ Ⓓ

LANGUAGE FOCUS

Verb Tenses

◎ 動詞の時制を確認しながら、次の英文を読んでみましょう。

1) Look! Here **comes** the train!
   ほら、列車が来ました。

2) I hear she's **got** a new boyfriend.
   彼女には新しい彼氏ができたらしいよ。

3) It's **been** five years since we **became** friends.
   私たちが友だちになって5年になる。

4) When **was** America **discovered** by Columbus?
   アメリカはいつコロンブスに発見されましたか。

5) We learned that water **boils** at 100℃.
   私たちは、水は摂氏100度で沸騰すると習った。

6) The Olympics and Paralympics **will be held** in Los Angeles in 2028.
   オリンピックとパラリンピックは2028年にロサンゼルスで開催される。

7) We'll go shopping if it **has stopped** raining by this afternoon.
   午後までに雨がやんだら、買い物に行きます。

INCOMPLETE SENTENCES

A word or phrase is missing in each of the sentences. Select the best answer to complete the sentence.

13. He _____ a book when his mother suddenly opened the door.

    (A) has read   (B) is reading   (C) reads   (D) was reading

14. We will have finished dinner by the time you _____ here.

    (A) did get   (B) get   (C) getting   (D) got

15. She said she _____ for Paris the following week.

    (A) leave   (B) leaves   (C) will leave   (D) would leave

16. According to the schedule, we _____ on a school trip next week.

    (A) go   (B) will be going   (C) will going   (D) would go

17. I _____ ill in bed since the day before yesterday.

    (A) am   (B) had been   (C) have been   (D) was

18. I _____ such a beautiful sunset before.

    (A) has never seen   (B) never have seen   (C) never saw   (D) never see

19. If I _____ bought the house, I would have more money now.

    (A) didn't   (B) don't   (C) hadn't   (D) haven't

20. I realized that I _____ my umbrella in his car.

    (A) have left   (B) had left   (C) leave   (D) left

21. We _____ each other for five years when we got married.

    (A) had known   (B) have known   (C) knew   (D) would know

22. I lost the eraser that I _____ the day before.

    (A) brought   (B) buy   (C) had bought   (D) have bought

23. I _____ the musical four times if I go with you tomorrow.

    (A) had seen   (B) have seen   (C) will have seen   (D) will see

PART 6 **TEXT COMPLETION**

Read the email that follows. A word or phrase is missing in some of the sentences. Select the best answer to complete the text.

From the Lending Counter, Central Library
Dear Mr. Sato (Student no.: 2201056)

___

This is to ____ you that an item you ____ on April 17th is now overdue. Please
 24 **25**
return it without delay. Details are shown below. Please be aware that penalties

are applicable when an item becomes 8 days overdue. These may ____ inellglblllty
 26
to borrow further items for a period and monetary fines. Details are available at

the Central Library website.

Please reply to this email or visit the Lending Counter directly if you have any

questions about this email.

Title: Read English Better!
Author: R. McDonald
Library Code: 823.1342 R21

---

24. (A) announce   (B) ask   (C) confirm   (D) inform

25. (A) borrowed   (B) have lent   (C) rented   (D) took

26. (A) consist   (B) exclude   (C) include   (D) intrude

Read the email that follows. Select the best answer for each question.

← ★ ↩ · · ·

TO: ALL UNDERGRADUATE STUDENTS
FROM: ACADEMIC AFFAIRS DIVISION

IMPORTANT NOTICE

This is to inform you of modifications to course registration rules that have come into effect this academic year.

Many language courses in the general undergraduate curriculum that have until now been open only to sophomores and above will now be open to all students, including freshmen. This change is intended to give students maximum flexibility in arranging their schedules and following their interests from their first year at college.

When choosing courses to take and deciding their timetables, students are advised to check that the level of any course that they wish to take is suitable. The level of each course is marked clearly in the course syllabus, listed in the Student Handbook and also available online through the Academic Affairs Division website. Students should also make themselves familiar with any additional registration guidelines of their academic department.

27. What is the purpose of this notice?
    (A) To encourage students to refer to departmental guidelines
    (B) To modify new course registration rules for sophomores and juniors
    (C) To tell students about new rules relating to language courses
    (D) To understand the levels of undergraduate language courses

28. What is the university trying to accomplish with this change?
    (A) To arrange the students' schedules with more flexibility
    (B) To encourage freshmen to learn from sophomores and juniors
    (C) To give students more choice
    (D) To make the Student Handbook easier to understand

29. What advice regarding course levels does the Academic Affairs Division give students?
    (A) To check whether the course is listed in the Student Handbook
    (B) To decide their timetable first and then discuss course levels with their academic tutor
    (C) To match the course level to their own level
    (D) To read the division's website frequently

30. What should students do in their departments?
    (A) They should check the guidelines.
    (B) They should familiarize departmental procedures.
    (C) They should follow the additional procedures.
    (D) They should go online to check whether the guidelines are reflected on the Academic Affairs Division website.

EATING & DRINKING

Match the words with their correct definitions.

(1) boiled ( )
(2) cafeteria ( )
(3) lunch box ( )
(4) meal ( )
(5) menu ( )
(6) order ( )
(7) reasonable ( )
(8) restaurant ( )
(9) skip ( )
(10) server ( )

(a) a container for a packed lunch
(b) a list of available dishes
(c) a place where you can drink tea or coffee and have a light meal
(d) a place where you can eat
(e) an occasion such as breakfast, lunch, or dinner
(f) cooked in hot water
(g) not very cheap and not too expensive
(h) someone who takes orders and serves food
(i) to ask for specific items from a menu
(j) to miss (e.g. a meal or class)

Have the following conversation with a partner, filling in the blanks from the box below. Then listen to the recording to check your answers and intonation.

A: Hello, sir, are you ready to _____?

B: No, I'm still _____. Could you give me a bit more _____?

A: Certainly, sir, I'll come _____ in a few minutes. ....

A: So, are you _____ now, sir?

B: Yes. I _____ I'll have the sirloin steak.

A: And how would you _____ it?

B: Rare, please.

| back | like | looking | order | ready | think | time |

PHOTOGRAPHS $\left(\frac{1}{06}\right)$

You will hear four short statements. Look at the picture and choose the statement that best describes what you see.

1.   Ⓐ Ⓑ Ⓒ Ⓓ

2.   Ⓐ Ⓑ Ⓒ Ⓓ

PART 2   **QUESTION–RESPONSE** $\left(\frac{1}{07}\right)$

You will hear a question or statement and three responses. Listen carefully, and choose the response to the question or statement.

3. Mark your answer.   Ⓐ Ⓑ Ⓒ

4. Mark your answer.   Ⓐ Ⓑ Ⓒ

5. Mark your answer.   Ⓐ Ⓑ Ⓒ

6. Mark your answer.   Ⓐ Ⓑ Ⓒ

PART 3 **SHORT CONVERSATIONS**

You will hear short conversations between two or more people. Listen carefully, and select the best response to each question.

Question 7 refers to the following conversation.

7. What are the speakers discussing?
   (A) The man's favorite food
   (B) The man's favorite restaurant
   (C) What the man wants to eat
   (D) Where the man is from

   Ⓐ Ⓑ Ⓒ Ⓓ

Question 8 refers to the following conversation.

8. What are the two speakers going to do?
   (A) The man doesn't want to go out.
   (B) They're going to a Chinese restaurant.
   (C) They're going to an Italian restaurant.
   (D) They're going to decide later.

   Ⓐ Ⓑ Ⓒ Ⓓ

Question 9 refers to the following conversation.

9. What's the problem?
   (A) The man wants more to eat.
   (B) The waiter brought the wrong food.
   (C) The woman is still hungry.
   (D) Their sandwiches don't taste good.

   Ⓐ Ⓑ Ⓒ Ⓓ

PART 4 **SHORT TALKS**

You will hear short talks given by a single speaker. Listen carefully, and select the best response to each question.

Question 10 refers to the following talk.

10. According to the speaker, which of the following statements is true?
    (A) Eating breakfast is not a good idea.
    (B) It is important to eat breakfast.
    (C) Many people don't like to eat or study.
    (D) You may skip breakfast if you are not hungry.

    Ⓐ Ⓑ Ⓒ Ⓓ

Question 11 refers to the following conversation.

11. What is the speaker talking about?
    - (A) Her favorite food
    - (B) Her lunch and dinner
    - (C) Love and hate
    - (D) Parents

Ⓐ Ⓑ Ⓒ Ⓓ

Question 12 refers to the following talk.

12. Who most likely is speaking?
    - (A) A customer
    - (B) A spokesperson
    - (C) A tour guide
    - (D) A server

Ⓐ Ⓑ Ⓒ Ⓓ

LANGUAGE FOCUS

Intransitive & Transitive Verbs

◎ 次の英文の（　　）内から、最も適当な語句を選んでください。

1) My father (listens, listens at, listens to) a podcast on his smartphone every evening.
   父は毎晩スマートフォンでポッドキャストを聞く。

2) The party (reached, reached at, reached to) the summit before sunrise.
   一行は日の出前に山頂に着いた。

3) I apologized (him, of him, to him) for being late.
   私は遅刻したことを彼に謝った。

4) Here are instructions for (accessing, accessing into, accessing to) the customer area of the website.
   ウェブサイトのお客様専用ページへのアクセスの仕方をご覧ください。

5) I stopped (eat, eating, to eat) lunch when my boss arrived.
   上司が到着したとき、私は昼食をやめた。

6) I agree (on, to, with) you that we should postpone the trip.
   旅行を延期すべきだというあなたの意見に賛成します。

7) Our boss enjoys (to make, making, of making) new marketing strategies.
   上司は、新しいマーケティング戦略を立てることを楽しんでいる。

A word or phrase is missing in each of the sentences. Select the best answer to complete the sentence.

13. I can't wait _____ this day to be over.
    (A) for   (B) in   (C) on   (D) to

14. His father _____ a bakery in front of the college.
    (A) runs   (B) runs at   (C) runs with   (D) runs without

15. Tom is looking for someone to drive _____ to the airport tomorrow.
    (A) he   (B) him   (C) his   (D) himself

16. George _____ in bed reading a magazine.
    (A) laid   (B) lay   (C) lie   (D) lied

17. My colleague _____ me about her work at lunch time.
    (A) complained (B) complained for (C) complained to (D) complained with

18. You had better not _____ that subject.
    (A) discuss   (B) discuss about   (C) to discuss   (D) to discuss about

19. She's _____ London for Tokyo in three days.
    (A) been left   (B) leaving   (C) leaving to   (D) left

20. The noise gets louder as you _____ the factory.
    (A) approach   (B) approach for   (C) approach to   (D) will approach

21. This type of smartphone _____ well in Japan.
    (A) is sold   (B) is being sold   (C) sell   (D) sells

22. I was _____ my sick mother when the phone rang.
    (A) attending at   (B) attending for   (C) attending on   (D) attending to

23. In old age, I am beginning to _____ my father.
    (A) resemble   (B) resemble like   (C) resemble to   (D) resemble with

Read the text that follows. A word or phrase is missing in some of the sentences. Select the best answer to complete the text.

WHOLE HEALTH RESTAURANT

The Whole Health Restaurant has recently reopened after extensive renovation work. Come and enjoy familiar dishes from our ____ past
                                                                                    24
as well as some new additions from our founder Jeff Clarkson's secret recipe book.

Our wholesome soups include lentil & cumin, carrot & ginger and gazpacho. In salads, try our tomatoes in raspberry vinegar with onion and mixed herbs. Our ____ range of delicious entrées features Middle
                              25
Eastern Chickpea Burgers and Slow-Cooked Swordfish with Creamy Fennel-Tomato Sauce.

In our famous and scrumptious dessert line-up, try Key Lime-Pie Cups, Apple Cranberry Crisp or Apricot & Strawberry Fool. All are low-calorie and low-fat. But your kids probably won't ____ that!
                                                                  26

24. (A) condescending　(B) confusing　(C) illustrious　(D) infamous

25. (A) exhausted　(B) expanded　(C) exploded　(D) extension

26. (A) concern　(B) notice　(C) notify　(D) regard

Questions 27–30 refer to the following review.

The Acropolis

Food: Very good
Price: Moderate
Service: Excellent
Decor: Very stylish
Location: 69 Atkins Lane, next to the theater
Opening hours: Lunch is available weekdays from 12:00 to 3:30, and 11:30 to 3:00 on the weekend. Dinner is available weekdays from 6:00 to 11:00, and 5:30 to 12:00 on weekends.
Recommended dishes: Lamb moussaka; Stifado beef stew; Apple pie with lemon sauce.
All major credit cards are accepted.

This is a nice place to come on weekends for local families with a modest budget who want to try something a little out of the ordinary. Although the Greek food is authentic, owner Stavros understands that kids may sometimes prefer American classics. A key feature that Stavros has maintained since the restaurant's establishment is that children under the age of 10 accompanying their families get a free dessert on weekday lunchtimes.

27. According to the reviewer, how are the prices at The Acropolis?
    (A) Expensive
    (B) High
    (C) Low
    (D) Reasonable

28. What dessert is recommended?

    (A) Apple pie
    (B) Chocolate and lemon ice cream
    (C) Chocolate cake
    (D) Lemon cake

29. Where would this review most likely be found?

    (A) In a window outside the restaurant
    (B) In an invitation to a birthday party dinner
    (C) In the business section of a newspaper
    (D) In the entertainment section of an online local newspaper

30. Which of the following is the best time for a family with young children to eat?

    (A) between 16:30 and 19:30 on Sundays
    (B) Saturdays between 18:00 and 20:00
    (C) Thursdays between 12:00 and 13:00
    (D) weekday evenings

WARM-UP (A)

Match the words with their correct definitions.

(1) agenda   (   )   (a) a document that summarizes information
(2) division   (   )   (b) a list of items for discussion
(3) document   (   )   (c) a place where business is carried out
(4) employment (   )   (d) a piece of writing that conveys information
(5) furniture   (   )   (e) an administrative unit of a business
(6) office   (   )   (f) items such as chairs and tables
(7) product   (   )   (g) money that a business makes beyond its costs
(8) profits   (   )   (h) work that you are paid to do
(9) report   (   )   (i) something sold by a business
(10) sales   (   )   (j) the quantity of goods sold by a company

WARM-UP (B)

Have the following conversation with a partner, filling in the blanks from the box below. Then listen to the recording to check your answers and intonation.

A: I think we need to have a _____ soon to discuss the annual results.

B: OK, how's your _____ next week?

A: I'm pretty booked up at the beginning of the week, but I have _____ free _____ towards the _____ of the week.

B: OK, how _____ Thursday morning?

A: OK, that _____ good.

| about | end | meeting | schedule | some | sounds | time |

18

PHOTOGRAPHS $\left(\frac{1}{10}\right)$

You will hear four short statements. Look at the picture and choose the statement that best describes what you see.

1.

Ⓐ Ⓑ Ⓒ Ⓓ

2.

Ⓐ Ⓑ Ⓒ Ⓓ

PART 2 **QUESTION-RESPONSE** $\left(\frac{1}{11}\right)$

You will hear a question or statement and three responses. Listen carefully, and choose the response to the question or statement.

3. Mark your answer.   Ⓐ Ⓑ Ⓒ

4. Mark your answer.   Ⓐ Ⓑ Ⓒ

5. Mark your answer.   Ⓐ Ⓑ Ⓒ

6. Mark your answer.   Ⓐ Ⓑ Ⓒ

SHORT CONVERSATIONS $\left(\frac{1}{12}\right)$

You will hear short conversations between two people. Listen carefully, and select the best response to each question.

Question 7 refers to the following conversation.

7.   What will the man and woman likely do this afternoon?

    (A) Check their email
    (B) Decide what the best idea is
    (C) Have a meeting
    (D) Work on a report   Ⓐ Ⓑ Ⓒ Ⓓ

Questions 8 through 9 refer to the following conversation.

8.   What is Simon's initial reaction to the annual results?

    (A) He feels confused.
    (B) He is angry.
    (C) He is generally satisfied.
    (D) He is very worried.   Ⓐ Ⓑ Ⓒ Ⓓ

9.   What is Jeanette worried about?

    (A) Global profits
    (B) Global sales
    (C) Sales in certain countries
    (D) The general state of the Chinese economy   Ⓐ Ⓑ Ⓒ Ⓓ

SHORT TALKS

You will hear a short talk given by a single speaker. Listen carefully, and select the best response to each question.

Question 10 refers to the following passage.

10. What will the man do today?

    (A) He got some basic information from his colleagues.
    (B) He will go to a shopping center.
    (C) He will look for a big project to work on.
    (D) He will work on a report.   Ⓐ Ⓑ Ⓒ Ⓓ

Questions 11 through 12 refer to the following passage.

11. At whom is this passage aimed?

    (A) At builders
    (B) At graphic artists and web designers
    (C) At people aiming to be secretaries
    (D) At students ⒶⒷⒸⒹ

12. How should those starting a new business choose a location?

    (A) They should buy a building to avoid paying rent.
    (B) They should find somewhere that clients will like.
    (C) They should find somewhere with cheap rent.
    (D) They should work from home to save money. ⒶⒷⒸⒹ

LANGUAGE FOCUS

Gerunds & Infinitives

◎ 次の英文の（　　）内から、最も適当な語句を選んでください。

1) I'm looking forward (see, seeing, to see, to seeing) you soon.
   まもなくあなたに会うのを楽しみにしています。

2) My grandmother lived (be, being, to be, to being) a hundred.
   私の祖母は100歳まで生きた。

3) I couldn't help (laugh, laughing, to laugh, to laughing).
   笑わずにはいられなかった。

4) I have no time (to worry, to worrying, worry, worrying) about things like that.
   そのようなことでくよくよしている時間はない。

5) Would you mind (tell, telling, to tell, told) me where your name comes from?
   お名前の由来を教えていただけませんでしょうか。

6) I put off (did, do, doing, to do) my homework until after the match.
   試合の後まで宿題をするのを先延ばしにした。

7) He admitted (break, broken, to break, to breaking) the law.
   彼はその法律を破ったのを認めた。

INCOMPLETE SENTENCES

A word or phrase is missing in each of the sentences. Select the best answer to complete the sentence.

13. The boys enjoyed _____ in the park yesterday.

    (A) play   (B) playing   (C) to play   (D) to playing

14. Remember _____ off your computer before leaving today.

    (A) to be turned   (B) to turn   (C) turning   (D) to turning

15. I gave up _____ after I saw a documentary on TV about its health consequences.

    (A) smoke   (B) smoked   (C) smoking   (D) to smoke

16. I considered _____ to college in the U.S., but I decided to study in Japan.

    (A) applying   (B) for me to apply   (C) my apply   (D) to apply

17. I will never forget _____ you for the first time.

    (A) meet   (B) meeting   (C) to meet   (D) to meeting

18. If you want to lose weight, you need to get used to _____ dessert.

    (A) deprived   (B) do without   (C) going into the   (D) going without

19. I gave up the chance _____ my favorite band live in order to study for my finals.

    (A) see   (B) seeing   (C) to see   (D) to listen

20. I remember someone _____ me that failure is inevitable so we should fail fast and fail often.

    (A) tell   (B) telling   (C) tells   (D) to tell

21. I hope _____ in software development after I graduate.

    (A) to work   (B) work   (C) working   (D) will work

22. How can we stop it _____ again?

    (A) happen   (B) happening   (C) to happen   (D) to happening

23. He's pretending not _____ even though he knows everything about the matter.

    (A) know   (B) knowing   (C) to know   (D) to knowing

TEXT COMPLETION

Read the text that follows. A word or phrase is missing in some of the sentences. Select the best answer to complete the text.

Questions 24–26 refer to the following email.

FROM: Manager, General Affairs
TO: All employees
DATE: March 10th, 20____
SUBJECT: Mr. Richard Carpenter's visit

Mr. Richard Carpenter, COO at our partner in the U.S., Stanton Enterprises, will be

visiting Tokyo next month, and will spend a large portion of his time here with us.

We have arranged a series of meetings and other events, detailed below. Please

make yourself _____ the arrangements so that you can participate as appropriate
        24

and show him the proper courtesy during his stay here.

On 3rd, soon after his arrival, we will have an informal reception here in the

offices. This will probably be around 3 p.m. but we will confirm the time on

the day. The reception will be in the main meeting room. Everyone not out on

business should attend. Those engaged in urgent work can just pay a quick

visit to say hello. If he is _____ his flight, we will call a halt after about an hour;
        25

otherwise, the reception may continue for some time.

On 4th, we will have a business meeting in the morning, at around 10 a.m. We

would like all section chiefs _____.
        26

---

24. (A) aware of   (B) beware of   (C) care for   (D) careful of

25. (A) exhausted at (B) tired from   (C) tired of   (D) weary

26. (A) attend   (B) attending   (C) attention   (D) to attend

Read the texts. Select the best answer for each question.

Questions 27 and 28 refer to the following text message chain.

Philip Simmonds:
Hi, Jean, running a bit late.

Jean Blair:
Are you going to make it in time for the meeting?

Philip Simmonds:
Don't think so. Sorry.

Jean Blair:
No worries. We can move the items that need your input to the end of the meeting.

Philip Simmonds:
Appreciate it.

Jean Blair:
How late do you think you're going to be?

Philip Simmonds:
About 30, I think. My train was late arriving at Penn Station so I didn't make my connection to New Brunswick.

Jean Blair:
Yes, that often happens on trains from Boston.

Philip Simmonds:
Anyway, better get to the platform. Later.

Jean Blair:
OK, see you when we see you.

---

27. What will Ms. Blair do to solve the problem discussed in the text messages?

    (A) Cancel the meeting
    (B) Postpone the meeting
    (C) Rearrange the items on the agenda
    (D) Remove the items concerning Mr. Simmonds from the agenda

28. What route is Mr. Simmonds taking?

    (A) Boston - Penn Station - New Brunswick
    (B) New Brunswick - Penn Station - Boston
    (C) Penn Station - Boston - New Brunswick
    (D) Penn Station - New Brunswick - Boston

Questions 29 and 30 refer to the following notice.

WANTED: Web Designer

A creative web designer urgently required to work on weekends. Must be creative and a team player. An interest in computer games would be good but is not essential. This is a good chance for students to get some experience before leaving school.

e-mail: info@games.com
web site: www.games.com

29. What skills are necessary for the job being advertised?
    (A) Baseball
    (B) Creativity and the ability to work in a team
    (C) Game design
    (D) The Java language

30. Who should respond to the advertisement?
    (A) Anyone who is available
    (B) People who have left school
    (C) People who can design games
    (D) Students with time on weekends

WARM-UP (A)

Match the words with their correct definitions.

(1)	blunt	( )	(a)	a powder usually made from wheat
(2)	chop	( )	(b)	a way to cook eggs
(3)	flour	( )	(c)	an implement used for cutting things
(4)	ingredients	( )	(d)	instructions for making a dish
(5)	insufficient	( )	(e)	not enough
(6)	knife	( )	(f)	not often
(7)	rarely	( )	(g)	the foods used to make a dish
(8)	raw	( )	(h)	the opposite of sharp
(9)	recipe	( )	(i)	to cut in small pieces
(10)	scramble	( )	(j)	uncooked

WARM-UP (B)

Have the following conversation with a partner, filling in the blanks from the box below. Then listen to the recording to check your answers and intonation.

A: _____ than going out to dinner, _____ don't we do some cooking tonight?

B: That's not a _____ idea. How about _____ some pizzas?

A: OK. The dough takes a _____ to rise, so we'd _____ get started.

B: Yes, I _____ you're right. Let's do it.

bad	better	guess	making	rather	while	why

PHOTOGRAPHS $\left(\frac{1}{14}\right)$

You will hear four short statements. Look at the picture and choose the statement that best describes what you see.

1.

(A) (B) (C) (D)

2.

(A) (B) (C) (D)

PART 2 **QUESTION-RESPONSE** $\left(\frac{1}{15}\right)$

You will hear a question or statement and three responses. Listen carefully, and choose the response to the question or statement.

3. Mark your answer.　　　　　　　　　　(A) (B) (C)

4. Mark your answer.　　　　　　　　　　(A) (B) (C)

5. Mark your answer.　　　　　　　　　　(A) (B) (C)

6. Mark your answer.　　　　　　　　　　(A) (B) (C)

You will hear short conversations between two or more people. Listen carefully, and select the best response to each question.

Question 7 refers to the following conversation.

7.   What are they making?

(A) A computer
(B) A steak
(C) A rice bowl
(D) Meringue   Ⓐ Ⓑ Ⓒ Ⓓ

Question 8 refers to the following conversation.

8.   What does the woman think about cooking videos online?

(A) She doesn't have an opinion.
(B) She thinks they are a complete solution.
(C) She thinks they are useful but insufficient.
(D) She thinks they are useless.   Ⓐ Ⓑ Ⓒ Ⓓ

Question 9 refers to the following conversation.

9.   What will the woman do now?

(A) It is not mentioned in the passage.
(B) She will check the fridge.
(C) She will cook a stew.
(D) She will go to the supermarket.   Ⓐ Ⓑ Ⓒ Ⓓ

You will hear short talks given by a single speaker. Listen carefully, and select the best response to each question.

Questions 10 through 11 refer to the following talk.

10. Which of the following is true?

(A) The speaker has a restaurant in the forest.
(B) The speaker has run a restaurant for seven years.
(C) The speaker's restaurant serves fish.
(D) The speaker likes to finish work early.   Ⓐ Ⓑ Ⓒ Ⓓ

11. Which of the following is NOT true?

   (A) Japanese people don't know much about Finnish food.
   (B) The food is probably suitable for Japanese people.
   (C) The restaurant is closed on Sundays.
   (D) The restaurant is very busy.

   (A) (B) (C) (D)

Question 12 refers to the following talk.

12. How does the speaker feel about cooking?

   (A) It is not clear from the talk.
   (B) She doesn't like it.
   (C) She likes it and does it often.
   (D) She likes it but rarely does it.

   (A) (B) (C) (D)

LANGUAGE FOCUS

Participles

◎ 次の英文の下線部に、(　　)内の動詞を適切な分詞に直して書き込んでください。

1) There is _____ support for his position. (increase)
   彼の立場への支持が増している。

2) Not _____ what to say, I kept silent. (know)
   何と言ったらいいか分からなかったので、黙っていた。

3) I got _____ with him at the party. (acquaint)
   私はパーティーで彼と知り合った。

4) I heard my name _____ from somewhere behind me. (call)
   私の名前が呼ばれるのが背後のどこからか聞こえた。

5) The art gallery requires all visitors to keep their cellphones
   _____ off. (turn)
   その美術館は全ての訪問者に携帯電話の電源を切っておくように求めている。

6) _____ from a plane, the island looks very beautiful. (see)
   飛行機から見ると、その島はとても美しく見える。

7) _____ by his expression, the project seems to be working.
   (judge)
   彼の表情から見て、プロジェクトはうまくいっているらしい。

A word or phrase is missing in each of the sentences. Select the best answer to complete the sentence.

13. He approached me, _____ brightly.

    (A) smiled   (B) smiles   (C) smiling   (D) to smile

14. He had me _____ in the rain for thirty minutes.

    (A) be waiting   (B) waited   (C) waiting   (D) to wait

15. I saw a little boy _____ by his mother.

    (A) been scolded   (B) being scolded   (C) scold   (D) scolding

16. The clothes _____ by young people have been changing these days.

    (A) to wear   (B) wearing   (C) wore   (D) worn

17. Employees _____ in the office after 6 p.m. should inform the security personnel when they leave.

    (A) intending stay (B) stayed   (C) staying   (D) to stay

18. No one I knew was at the party and I felt quite _____.

    (A) bore   (B) bored   (C) boring   (D) born

19. She stood still with her eyes _____ on a painting.

    (A) fix   (B) fixed   (C) fixing   (D) to fix

20. _____ what to say, she kept silent.

    (A) As knowing   (B) Didn't know   (C) Knowing not   (D) Not knowing

21. It _____ Monday, the barber shop was closed.

    (A) be   (B) been   (C) being   (D) was

22. Generally _____, there is a tendency to read less and less these days.

    (A) speak   (B) speaking   (C) spoken   (D) to speak

23. Before we launch the project, we have to create a consensus among those _____.

    (A) concern   (B) concerned   (C) concerning   (D) to concern

Read the text that follows. A word or phrase is missing in some of the sentences. Select the best answer to complete the text.

Questions 24–26 refer to the following article.

Lemon meringue pie is a little tricky to make, but it's not too _____ if

24

you think about it in three parts. First, you make the pie crust by

mixing biscuit crumbs with melted butter, and put the pie crust in the

_____ to cool and become harder. Then, for the lemon pie filling, you

25

mix sugar, flour, water, lemon juice, and lemon zest. To make meringue,

you basically just whisk egg whites, trying to get as much air in there

_____, and gradually fold in sugar. If you try it two or three times at

26

home, I'm sure you'll become good at it.

---

24. (A) constant   (B) difficult   (C) easy   (D) enjoyable

25. (A) computer   (B) fire   (C) oven   (D) refrigerator

26. (A) as possible   (B) can be   (C) he likes   (D) very easy

Questions 27 through 30 refer to the following recipe and text message chain. Select the best answer for each question.

Mama Steinberg's Cranberry Relish

2 cups whole raw cranberries, washed
1 small onion
3/4 cup sour cream
1/2 cup sugar
2 tablespoons prepared horseradish

Chop the raw berries and onion and mix in a food processor. Add remaining ingredients and mix. Put in a plastic container and freeze. Prepare Thanksgiving morning and let sit one hour before serving. Makes 1–1 1/2 pints.

Bess Crampton:
Hey, Jeanette, do you have a moment to help me with that recipe you gave me?

Jeanette Lewis:
Sure, what's the problem?

Bess Crampton:
I think I followed all the instructions correctly but it seems more watery than I imagined.

Jeanette Lewis:
Well, it is a relish. You may be thinking of cranberry jelly. That's what many people are used to. The cranberries are cooked so it becomes like a jam. For the relish we use raw cranberries. Have you tried it yet?

Bess Crampton:
No, I kind of panicked when it looked different from what I imagined. Let me try now.

Bess Crampton:
Oh, it's wonderful. Sorry to trouble you!

Jeanette Lewis:
No problem! Glad it worked out!

27. When would this relish be served?

    (A) Christmas Day
    (B) Easter Day
    (C) Labor Day
    (D) Thanksgiving Day

28. What is NOT included in the recipe?

    (A) cranberries
    (B) strawberries
    (C) sour cream
    (D) onion

29. Why does Bess Crampton text Jeanette Lewis?

    (A) She doesn't have enough cranberry relish.
    (B) She expected the cranberry relish to be harder.
    (C) She thinks the cranberry relish is too hard.
    (D) The cranberry relish doesn't taste good.

30. What is the nature of Bess Crampton's misunderstanding?

    (A) She confused cranberry jelly and cranberry relish.
    (B) She cooked the cranberries by mistake.
    (C) She didn't use enough cranberries.
    (D) She used the wrong ingredients.

WARM-UP Ⓐ

Match the words with their correct definitions.

(1) doctor ( )
(2) exhaustion ( )
(3) fever ( )
(4) hospitalize ( )
(5) medication ( )
(6) nutritionist ( )
(7) patient ( )
(8) prescribe ( )
(9) saturated fat ( )
(10) treatment ( )

(a) a high body temperature
(b) a kind of fat found in meat, coconut, and other foods
(c) a professional who gives advice on healthy eating
(d) a state of extreme tiredness
(e) medical care in general
(f) a drug given to someone who is sick
(g) someone receiving medical care
(h) someone who diagnoses disease and gives advice on treatment
(i) to commit someone to a stay in hospital
(j) to give written advice on medicines to be taken

WARM-UP Ⓑ

Have the following conversation with a partner, filling in the blanks from the box below. Then listen to the recording to check your answers and intonation.

A: Hello, Mr. Smith. What _____ I do for you?

B: Well, doctor, I have a slight _____.

A: How long has this been _____ on?

B: Two or three _____ now.

A: I'd better take a _____ at you then. …Mmm, I can't see anything _____. Maybe we'd better do some _____.

| can | fever | going | look | tests | weeks | wrong |

You will hear four short statements. Look at the picture and choose the statement that best describes what you see.

1.  Ⓐ Ⓑ Ⓒ Ⓓ

2.  Ⓐ Ⓑ Ⓒ Ⓓ

PART 2 **QUESTION–RESPONSE**

You will hear a question or statement and three responses. Listen carefully, and choose the response to the question or statement.

3. Mark your answer. Ⓐ Ⓑ Ⓒ

4. Mark your answer. Ⓐ Ⓑ Ⓒ

5. Mark your answer. Ⓐ Ⓑ Ⓒ

6. Mark your answer. Ⓐ Ⓑ Ⓒ

You will hear short conversations between two people. Listen carefully, and select the best response to each question.

Question 7 refers to the following conversation.

7.   What is the man's problem?

(A) He does not like his job.
(B) He is lost.
(C) He is not well.
(D) His fever has gotten worse.   Ⓐ Ⓑ Ⓒ Ⓓ

Questions 8 and 9 refer to the following conversation.

8.   Why is the woman concerned?

(A) She thinks the man looks tired.
(B) The hospital is full.
(C) The man gives an incorrect answer to a question.
(D) The man is angry with her.   Ⓐ Ⓑ Ⓒ Ⓓ

9.   What kind of difficult situation is the man facing?

(A) He has to do the work of his boss.
(B) He has to stay in the hospital for some time.
(C) He is disappointed because he is not going to be promoted.
(D) He needs to fill in for someone for one week.   Ⓐ Ⓑ Ⓒ Ⓓ

PART 4   **SHORT TALKS**

You will hear short talks given by a single speaker. Listen carefully, and select the best response to each question.

Question 10 refers to this extract from an orientation meeting.

10. What kind of restriction is mentioned in the e-mail?

(A) The drugs that doctors can prescribe
(B) The length of hospitalization
(C) The total cost of treatment
(D) Which hospitals employees can use   Ⓐ Ⓑ Ⓒ Ⓓ

Question 11 refers to the following announcement.

11. Who is the message addressed to?

    (A) Matthew
    (B) Matthew's mother and father
    (C) Matthew's son
    (D) The people at the information desk   Ⓐ Ⓑ Ⓒ Ⓓ

Question 12 refers to the following talk.

12. Who is Pat Jennings?

    (A) He is an assistant to the company president.
    (B) He is the Chief Medical Officer at the company.
    (C) He is the president of the company.
    (D) He works for the municipal health department.   Ⓐ Ⓑ Ⓒ Ⓓ

LANGUAGE FOCUS

Phrasal Verbs

◎ 下の日本語の意味を表すように、次の英文の（　　）内に適語を入れてください。

1) Don't put (　　　　　　　　) till tomorrow what you can do today.
   今日できることは明日まで延ばすな。

2) I ran as fast as possible to catch up (　　　　　　　) her.
   彼女に追いつくためにできるだけ早く走った。

3) The police are trying to do (　　　　　　) with crime.
   警察は犯罪をなくそうと努めている。

4) We're looking forward (　　　　　　) seeing you again.
   私たちはあなたとの再会を楽しみにしています。

5) He is looked (　　　　　) to as our leader.
   彼は私たちのリーダーとして尊敬されている。

6) If you don't know the meaning of a word, look it (　　　　　　) in a
   dictionary.
   単語の意味が分からないなら、辞書を引きなさい。

7) 両親とはうまくいっていますか。
   Do you get along well (　　　　　　) your parents?

INCOMPLETE SENTENCES

A word or phrase is missing in each of the sentences. Select the best answer to complete the sentence.

13. Did you _____ up with an idea for a new product?

    (A) become   (B) come   (C) go   (D) take

14. His mother asked him to _____ his younger sister while she went shopping.

    (A) give up   (B) hang out   (C) look after   (D) take care

15. I've already _____ money this month.

    (A) been down on   (B) come down from   (C) gone through with
    (D) run out of

16. Please refrain _____ tap water.

    (A) away drinking   (B) drinking   (C) from drinking   (D) to drinking

17. You need to _____ your sorrows and get on with your life.

    (A) get back   (B) get out   (C) get over   (D) get up

18. Dr. Smith is flying back to London tonight. Shall I _____?

    (A) call her up   (B) greet her goodbye   (C) see her off   (D) send her back

19. How do you _____ your success?

    (A) account for   (B) deal with   (C) insist on   (D) work out

20. What were you _____ to say back there?

    (A) about   (B) doing   (C) suppose   (D) supposing

21. I tried to _____ the cockroaches, but they keep coming back.

    (A) do away   (B) garbage off with   (C) get rid of   (D) trash out

22. Our company is well placed to _____ current trends.

    (A) benefit   (B) get use of   (C) make benefit from   (D) take advantage of

23. The president can't come. Do you want to go ahead with the meeting or _____?

    (A) call it off   (B) cancel it through   (C) deem it through   (D) drop it off

Read the text that follows. A word or phrase is missing in some of the sentences. Select the best answer to complete the text.

Questions 24–26 refer to the following notice.

HEALTHWISE GYM & SPORTS CLUB: OPENING SOON! SPECIAL OFFER

Healthwise Gym & Sports Club will be opening at the beginning of August.

Get half off your first year's membership by joining ____ the end of July. We
24

offer the only comprehensive service and sports service in the downtown

area. If you haven't checked us out yet, visit our website. Here are some of our

services:

· General-purpose rooms that local sports groups can ____ by the hour at
25

   reasonable rates for regular practice sessions, tournaments, etc.

· A training room with a comprehensive selection of weights and exercise

   machines, with expert trainers ____ to give you advice
26

· Table tennis facilities, and badminton, basketball, and volleyball courts

Visit *www.healthwisegym.com* for more details or to join!

24. (A) by   (B) during   (C) until   (D) when

25. (A) borrow   (B) buy   (C) lend   (D) rent

26. (A) by all means (B) by side   (C) occupied   (D) on hand

Read the text and select the best answer for each question.

Questions 27–30 refer to the following text.

NUTRITION WORKSHOP

Are you a registered nutritionist who has been in the job for 10 years? Are you a physician who wants to be able to give patients advice other than when to take their medications? If so, we recommend that you find the time to attend these workshops. They will give you up-to-date information, some of which may surprise you.

Do you often advise patients to take supplemental calcium?
Do you sometimes advise patients to switch from butter to margarine to reduce their saturated fat intake?
Do you advise patients to give up nuts because they are high in calories?

If you answered Yes to any of these questions, you may not be doing your patients any favors. The first piece of advice may damage the mineral balance in their bodies, the second increases intake of trans-fats, which are more harmful than saturated fats, and the third may deprive them of a whole range of useful nutrients, including Omega-3 fatty acids. Attend the workshops and bring your knowledge up to date. Based on the latest findings in nutritional medicine, they will give you solid knowledge of recent research and the confidence to answer your patients' questions.

To accommodate medical personnel's varied schedules, we will hold the same workshop on four separate occasions:

Session 1:   July 3rd, 08:00–12:00
Session 2:   July 4th, 14:00–18:00
Session 3:   July 6th, 08:00–12:00
Session 4:   July 7th, 14:00–18:00

Email the address shown below to book your place, and to receive a certificate of attendance after the workshop.

Lecturer: Philip Weston, M.D., Ph.D.
Chief Scientist, Routledge Center for Nutritional Sciences

27. At whom are the workshops aimed?

    (A) At all medical personnel with more than ten years' experience

    (B) At anyone interested in nutritional science

    (C) At doctors

    (D) At medical personnel with an interest in nutrition

28. What opinion is expressed regarding butter?

    (A) It has too many trans-fats.

    (B) It is not as bad as margarine.

    (C) It should be eliminated.

    (D) It should be replaced by margarine.

29. What is said regarding nuts?

    (A) Only a nut would eat them.

    (B) They are a source of useful nutrients.

    (C) They do not contain fatty acids.

    (D) They will not be discussed in the workshops.

30. Which of the following will people attending the workshops get?

    (A) A certificate of attendance

    (B) Greater confidence in their medical technique

    (C) Knowledge of the history of nutritional science

    (D) Sixteen hours' worth of up-to-date knowledge

6 SHOPPING

WARM-UP (A)

Match the words with their correct definitions.

(1) apologize   (   )   (a) a fixed way of doing something
(2) branch   (   )   (b) a large building containing many shops
(3) credit card (   )   (c) a local shop belonging to a larger company
(4) discount   (   )   (d) a period of time in which prices are reduced
(5) empty   (   )   (e) a price reduction
(6) mall   (   )   (f) a way to pay for things
(7) picturesque (   )   (g) pretty
(8) prefer   (   )   (h) the opposite of full
(9) procedure   (   )   (i) to like something more than something else
(10) sale   (   )   (j) to say sorry

WARM-UP (B)

Have the following conversation with a partner, filling in the blanks from the box below. Then listen to the recording to check your answers and intonation.

A: Have you been to the sale _____?

B: _____ sale are you _____ about?

A: The one at Hiptown Mall. Didn't you _____?

B: No. What's so _____ about it?

A: Well, some stores are _____ the mall, and they have _____ re-
    ductions on all their goods.

know	leaving	massive	special	talking	what	yet

PHOTOGRAPHS

You will hear four short statements. Look at the picture and choose the statement that best describes what you see.

1.

Ⓐ Ⓑ Ⓒ Ⓓ

2.

Ⓐ Ⓑ Ⓒ Ⓓ

PART 2 **QUESTION-RESPONSE**

You will hear a question or statement and three responses. Listen carefully, and choose the response to the question or statement.

3. Mark your answer.   Ⓐ Ⓑ Ⓒ

4. Mark your answer.   Ⓐ Ⓑ Ⓒ

5. Mark your answer.   Ⓐ Ⓑ Ⓒ

6. Mark your answer.   Ⓐ Ⓑ Ⓒ

PART 3   SHORT CONVERSATIONS   ($\frac{1}{24}$)

You will hear short conversations between two people. Listen carefully, and select the best response to each question.

Question 7 refers to the following conversation.

7. Where did the man get his sweater?

    (A) A friend said it looked great.
    (B) He sent it as a gift.
    (C) His friend gave it to him.
    (D) His mother sent it to him.   Ⓐ Ⓑ Ⓒ Ⓓ

Question 8 refers to the following conversation.

8. When does the store close?

    (A) At 10 a.m.
    (B) At 10 p.m.
    (C) On Sundays
    (D) It depends on the day.   Ⓐ Ⓑ Ⓒ Ⓓ

Question 9 refers to the following conversation.

9. Why is the man surprised?

    (A) Central Shopping Mall has so many sales.
    (B) The sale is so long.
    (C) The woman is carrying many bags.
    (D) The woman's bag is very big.   Ⓐ Ⓑ Ⓒ Ⓓ

PART 4   SHORT TALKS   ($\frac{1}{25}$)

You will hear short talks given by a single speaker. Listen carefully, and select the best response to each question.

Question 10 refers to the following talk.

10. What floor are the toys on?

    (A) the first floor
    (B) the second floor
    (C) the third floor
    (D) the fourth floor   Ⓐ Ⓑ Ⓒ Ⓓ

Questions 11 through 12 refer to the following announcement.

11. When will the winter sale end?

    (A) At the end of the month

    (B) Immediately

    (C) In two days' time

    (D) Tomorrow   Ⓐ Ⓑ Ⓒ Ⓓ

12. In which department can you get discounts of 50%?

    (A) In all departments

    (B) In Interior

    (C) In Men's Clothing

    (D) In Women's Clothing   Ⓐ Ⓑ Ⓒ Ⓓ

LANGUAGE FOCUS

More Verb Questions

◎ 動詞の使い方を確認しながら、次の英文を読んでください。

1) Although it was raining, I **decided** *to take* a walk.
   雨が降っていたが、散歩することにした。

2) If you **want** some more of this wine, I *will send* you some.
   このワインがもっと欲しいなら、送ってあげるよ。

3) If you **will forgive** me, I *will tell* you the truth.
   もしあなたが私を許してくれるのであれば、本当のことを話します。

4) Please **make** *yourself* at home and **help** *yourself* to some coffee.
   どうぞご自由におくつろぎになって、コーヒーを自由にお飲みください。

5) I **have been asked** to *give* you a letter from him.
   彼からあなたに手紙を渡すように頼まれた。

6) You **are** not **allowed** *to drink* because you are under age.
   あなたは未成年なので飲酒は許されていない。

7) **Were** I in your position, I *would accept* his offer.
   私があなたの立場なら、彼の提案を受け入れる。

INCOMPLETE SENTENCES

A word or phrase is missing in each of the sentences. Select the best answer to complete the sentence.

13. What's _____ at the movie theater now?

(A) played   (B) playing   (C) plays   (D) to play

14. Mark, together with his friends, _____ going to the museum on Saturday.

(A) are   (B) has   (C) have   (D) is

15. Nothing interesting ever _____ around here.

(A) happens   (B) is happened   (C) happening   (D) are happened

16. Her new book is going to _____ next month.

(A) be publishing   (B) be published   (C) publish   (D) publishing

17. I decided that I _____ in the U.S.

(A) am studying   (B) study   (C) studied   (D) would study

18. I'll finish my homework before my brother _____ back.

(A) come   (B) comes   (C) is coming   (D) will come

19. Simon _____ to substitute for Paul in the soccer match.

(A) asked   (B) asks   (C) was asked   (D) will ask

20. Please _____ me to buy more bread for breakfast.

(A) remembrance   (B) remember   (C) remembering   (D) remind

21. Many places _____ by the floods that swept through the area.

(A) damage   (B) damaged   (C) was damaged   (D) were damaged

22. I deeply _____ your kindness.

(A) apply   (B) appreciate   (C) thank   (D) thank for

23. I _____ a car from my friend.

(A) borrowed   (B) gave   (C) lent   (D) was borrowed

TEXT COMPLETION

Read the text that follows. A word or phrase is missing in some of the sentences. Select the best answer to complete the text.

Questions 24–26 refer to the following letter.

October 15th

Dear Ms. Cortez,

I am writing to apologize for the mistake we made with your order ____
                                                                    24
August 22nd. Normally our staff take pains to read each order carefully

and fill it exactly as requested by the customer.

Our normal procedures clearly did not work in the case of your order,

and as a result you received a bag that was not only the wrong color

but also the wrong size. After your initial complaint, we sent you a bag

of the correct size, but again got the color slightly wrong. ___, you are
                                                              25
still to receive the bag you ordered. I can assure you that one is on its

way to you now.

Normally, we ask customers to send back items that do not ___ their
                                                           26
needs. Because of our repeated mistakes, however, I would like to

invite you to keep the bag currently in your possession and also enjoy

the use of the bag currently on its way to you.

My apologies again, and I hope this resolves things to your satisfaction.

Robert Edwards
Customer Service Manager
California Bags, Ltd.

---

24. (A) data   (B) date   (C) dated   (D) dating

25. (A) Because   (B) Consequently (C) Incidentally (D) The result

26. (A) accord   (B) conform   (C) meet   (D) require

Read the text that follows. Select the best answer for each question and mark the letter (A), (B), (C), or (D).

Questions 27–30 refer to the following notice.

Come and Celebrate the Opening of River City!

The largest shopping mall in Springfield is opening this Saturday. Featuring branches of internationally-renowned stores and locally owned boutiques and located on a picturesque, 150,000-square-meter site along the bank of the River Dart, just 5km outside of the town, it's an ideal place to go when you want to treat yourself.

It's not all shopping! With a large selection of restaurants and cafés, and with free seating areas in four locations, there are plenty of opportunities to relax. The Riverside Open-Air Theater features a range of entertainments throughout the day seven days a week, and live performances by local musicians in the evenings from Friday through Tuesday. Wednesday evenings will feature plays by Springfield City Theater Troupe.

On Opening Weekend only, enjoy a 10% discount on all items in all stores!

Open 7 days a week, 10:00 A.M. – 10:00 P.M. (Some stores close earlier.)

27. When will River City open?

    (A) Next month
    (B) The coming Wednesday
    (C) The coming weekend
    (D) Today

28. Where is River City?

    (A) It is in Springfield City Center.
    (B) It is near the Springfield City Theater.
    (C) It is next to the River Dart.
    (D) It is spread across four locations.

29. When will there be events at the Riverside Open-Air Theater?

   (A) Every day
   (B) Every evening except on weekends
   (C) Every evening except Thursday
   (D) Every evening except Tuesday

30. When and where will a 10% discount apply?

   (A) For the first two days on all items
   (B) For the first two days on selected items
   (C) For the opening week on all items
   (D) For the opening week on selected items

WARM-UP Ⓐ

Match the words with their correct definitions.

(1)	emergency	( )	(a)	a charged particle
(2)	fridge	( )	(b)	a drama in which people suffer or die
(3)	ignore	( )	(c)	a kitchen appliance used to keep things cold
(4)	innovative	( )	(d)	a written work intended to be performed on stage
(5)	ion	( )	(e)	an object used to protect people from the rain
(6)	negative	( )	(f)	based on old ways or beliefs
(7)	play	( )	(g)	of great originality
(8)	traditional	( )	(h)	something requiring an immediate response
(9)	tragedy	( )	(i)	the opposite of positive
(10)	umbrella	( )	(j)	to fail to pay attention to something

WARM-UP Ⓑ

Have the following conversation with a partner, filling in the blanks from the box below. Then listen to the recording to check your answers and intonation.

A: What are you _____ this weekend?

B: My family are going _____.

A: That sounds _____. But won't it _____ a bit cold?

B: Maybe a little. But we have _____ sleeping bags. And the site gets _____ crowded as summer approaches.

A: Well, I _____ you have a good time.

be	camping	doing	hope	nice	really	warm

PHOTOGRAPHS $\left(\frac{1}{26}\right)$

You will hear four short statements. Look at the picture and choose the statement that best describes what you see.

1.  Ⓐ Ⓑ Ⓒ Ⓓ

2.  Ⓐ Ⓑ Ⓒ Ⓓ

PART 2 **QUESTION-RESPONSE** $\left(\frac{1}{27}\right)$

You will hear a question or statement and three responses. Listen carefully, and choose the response to the question or statement.

3. Mark your answer. Ⓐ Ⓑ Ⓒ

4. Mark your answer. Ⓐ Ⓑ Ⓒ

5. Mark your answer. Ⓐ Ⓑ Ⓒ

6. Mark your answer. Ⓐ Ⓑ Ⓒ

PART 3   SHORT CONVERSATIONS

You will hear a short conversation between two people. Listen carefully, and select the best response to each question.

Questions 7 through 9 refer to the following conversation.

7. Why is Olivia calling Augustana?
   (A) To cancel their plans
   (B) To change the time of their appointment
   (C) To invite her to her house
   (D) To suggest that they go shopping together   (A) (B) (C) (D)

8. What is Augustana doing now?
   (A) She is buying some cakes.
   (B) She is returning some cakes that were not satisfactory.
   (C) She is shopping at the supermarket.
   (D) She is waiting for Olivia.   (A) (B) (C) (D)

9. What will Augustana and Olivia likely do?
   (A) They will meet at Augustana's house.
   (B) They will meet at Olivia's house.
   (C) They will meet at the cake shop.
   (D) They will meet at the supermarket.   (A) (B) (C) (D)

PART 4   SHORT TALKS

You will hear short talks given by a single speaker. Listen carefully, and select the best response to each question.

Question 10 refers to the following telephone message.

10. What does the caller want?
    (A) She wants Mr. Lopez to call her on Wednesday.
    (B) She wants Mr. Lopez to call her today.
    (C) She wants Mr. Lopez to change his reservation.
    (D) She wants to apologize for failing to book the seats Mr. Lopez wanted.
       (A) (B) (C) (D)

Question 11 refers to the following telephone message.

11. What does Ms. Swinton want?
    (A) She wants Barry to stop coming to school.
    (B) She wants Mr. and Ms. Walker to take Barry home.
    (C) She wants Mr. and Ms. Walker to wait at home.
    (D) She wants to take Barry to the emergency room at the hospital.
       (A) (B) (C) (D)

Question 12 refers to the following telephone message.

12. Why is Jerry calling Mr. Gonzalez?
   (A) He wants to apologize for the damage he has caused to Mr. Gonzalez's car.
   (B) Jerry has obtained the parts Mr. Gonzalez needs.
   (C) Mr. Gonzalez's car is ready to be picked up.
   (D) The repairs Mr. Gonzalez's car needs may be expensive.   Ⓐ Ⓑ Ⓒ Ⓓ

LANGUAGE FOCUS

Adjectives & Adverbs

◎ 次の英文を読んで、形容詞と副詞がどのように使われているか確認しましょう。

1) Do you have anything **cold** to drink?
   何か冷たい飲み物はありますか。

2) Why do you **always** look **so serious**?
   どうしていつもそんなに深刻な顔をしているのですか。

3) I'd like my steak **medium**, please.
   ステーキはミディアムにしてください。

4) Please speak **quietly** while my baby is sleeping.
   赤ん坊が寝ている間はどうか静かに話してください。

5) That's a **reasonably priced** restaurant, and the food is **extremely good**.
   あそこは手ごろな値段のレストランだが、食べ物はすごく良い。

6) My daughter learns languages **incredibly quickly**.
   娘は信じられないくらい早く言葉を覚える。

7) The kid is **completely** out of control.
   あの子はまったく手に負えない。

A word or phrase is missing in each of the sentences. Select the best answer to complete the sentence.

13. Although she liked to eat Chinese food at least once a month, she _____ liked Italian food.

    (A) also   (B) but   (C) only   (D) too

14. I'd like to go with you, but I'm afraid I don't have _____ time.

    (A) enough   (B) insufficient   (C) plenty   (D) too

15. Be _____ to bring your umbrella with you in case it rains.

    (A) certainly   (B) sure   (C) surely   (D) surer

16. The knife is _____, so we have to be careful when we handle it.

    (A) black   (B) dull   (C) long   (D) sharp

17. The computer desk is _____ the window in my office.

    (A) above   (B) next to   (C) over   (D) through

18. If you _____ know the answer to the question, you can go on to the next question.

    (A) almost   (B) already   (C) still   (D) yet

19. Her new comic book is _____ more amusing than the previous ones.

    (A) much   (B) too   (C) very   (D) well

20. It is a _____ opportunity to study abroad and experience foreign culture.

    (A) good   (B) much   (C) very   (D) well

21. The student was _____ for the exam this morning.

    (A) late   (B) lately   (C) lateness   (D) later

22. He _____ ever studies, except before exams.

    (A) does   (B) often   (C) hardly   (D) increasingly

23. If you have a car, you can go there _____.

    (A) ease   (B) easily   (C) easy   (D) uneasy

TEXT COMPLETION

Read the text that follows. A word or phrase is missing in some of the sentences. Select the best answer to complete the text.

Questions 24–26 refer to the following notice on a website.

Finding it difficult to make ends meet? If you work a regular nine-to-five job, you may be ignoring your earning potential. Do you have a skill ____
24
accounting or translating a foreign language?

When an employee leaves a company, or when an unexpected surge of orders comes in, companies often cannot cope just with their existing staff and they have a need for extra help. Our business at Hampton Enterprises is to put them ____ people like you.
25
How does it work? First, you register with us, giving us your interests and skills, general availability, and bank account details for us to pay you.

Then, when a job comes up that fits your profile, we email you. You look at the job and, if it suits you, we agree on a timeline for delivery of the finished product. We pay you at the end of every month for all the work ____ in the
26
previous month.

So what are you waiting for? Start earning a little extra today!

---

24. (A) either   (B) ex.   (C) for   (D) such as

25. (A) contacting   (B) in touch with   (C) through   (D) with regards to

26. (A) competition   (B) completed   (C) completing   (D) completion

Read the text that follows. Select the best answer for each question and mark the letter (A), (B), (C), or (D).

Questions 27–30 refer to the following invitation.

From the Levenson Memorial Office, Marsden University

You are cordially invited to attend
the 9th Levenson Memorial Lecture, to be conducted by
Dr. Priti Anand
and entitled
Are Humans Alone in the Universe?
on March 18th, 20___
in the Hansard Lecture Theater.

As I am sure you are aware, Dr. Anand is University Distinguished Professor of Astronomy at Marsden University. Her first book *Life Itself* broke all nonfiction sales records. She is known worldwide for her innovative theories on the nature of the Universe and the processes that lead to the development of life. She is the author of other popular bestsellers *Are We Alone?* and *What is Astronomy?*, as well as numerous respected scientific papers such as *The Development of Life* and various monographs. She is renowned for her lively and engaging lecturing style which has endeared her both to her students at Marsden and to her numerous fans among the general public.

The Levenson Memorial Lectures are annual events designed to engage the wider public well beyond the ivory tower in the intellectual life of the nation. In their nearly one decade of history, they have seen the leading scholars of our times come to Marsden and involve us all in the major issues of our age. Look out also for announcements regarding special events leading up to the 10th-anniversary lecture scheduled for next year.

Please note that entry is free of charge. RSVP by March 1st at levenson_memorial@marsden.edu or register online at levenson.marsden.edu using your registration code 042-5726. For cancelations only, please call (525) 312-2222.

We hope you are able to attend.

27. Which of the following is NOT a book by Professor Anand?

   (A) Are We Alone?
   (B) Life Itself
   (C) The Development of Life
   (D) What is Astronomy?

28. The word "engaging" in paragraph 1 is closest in meaning to

   (A) abstract
   (B) boring
   (C) controversial
   (D) fascinating

29. What is the purpose of the Levenson Memorial Lectures?

   (A) To develop innovative theories
   (B) To get all the staff at Marsden University interested in issues beyond the college
   (C) To increase interest among the general public in intellectual matters
   (D) To raise funds for repairs at Marsden University

30. How should the recipient of the invitation register?

   (A) By e-mail
   (B) By e-mail or online
   (C) By e-mail, online, or by phone
   (D) Registration is unnecessary.

WARM-UP Ⓐ

Match the words with their correct definitions.

(1)	budget	( )	(a)	a document distributed in meetings or classes	
(2)	clarify	( )	(b)	a kind of customer	
(3)	client	( )	(c)	a plan for spending money	
(4)	email	( )	(d)	a portable computer	
(5)	fruitful	( )	(e)	a tool for electronic communication	
(6)	handout	( )	(f)	a way of thinking about things	
(7)	laptop	( )	(g)	happening four times a year	
(8)	participant	( )	(h)	producing good results	
(9)	perspective	( )	(i)	someone who takes part in something	
(10)	quarterly	( )	(j)	to make something clearer	

WARM-UP Ⓑ

Have the following conversation with a partner, filling in the blanks from the box below. Then listen to the recording to check your answers and intonation.

A: Hey, I _____ you got a promotion. Congratulations!

B: Oh, _____.

A: What's the new job _____?

B: To be _____, I don't _____ like it. There are so many meetings.

A: Oh no. Well, I'm _____ you'll get _____ to it eventually.

heard	honest	like	really	sure	thanks	used

PHOTOGRAPHS

You will hear four short statements. Look at the picture and choose the statement that best describes what you see.

1. 　　　　　　　Ⓐ Ⓑ Ⓒ Ⓓ

2. 　　　　　　　Ⓐ Ⓑ Ⓒ Ⓓ

PART 2　　# QUESTION-RESPONSE

You will hear a question or statement and three responses. Listen carefully, and choose the response to the question or statement.

3.　Mark your answer.　　　　　　Ⓐ Ⓑ Ⓒ

4.　Mark your answer.　　　　　　Ⓐ Ⓑ Ⓒ

5.　Mark your answer.　　　　　　Ⓐ Ⓑ Ⓒ

6.　Mark your answer.　　　　　　Ⓐ Ⓑ Ⓒ

SHORT CONVERSATIONS

$\left(\frac{1}{32}\right)$

You will hear a short conversation between two people. Listen carefully, and select the best response to each question.

Question 7 refers to the following conversation.

7. What does Bill think about the company's strategy?
    (A) He worries that staff will not stay at the company unless salaries are raised.
    (B) He thinks the company needs to expand more aggressively.
    (C) He thinks the company should focus more on local customers.
    (D) He thinks that the company takes his ideas for granted.   Ⓐ Ⓑ Ⓒ Ⓓ

Questions 8 and 9 refer to the following conversation.

8. What is Casey doing?
    (A) Changing a schedule
    (B) Checking the availability of rooms
    (C) Checking the monthly budget
    (D) Waiting for a 10 o'clock meeting   Ⓐ Ⓑ Ⓒ Ⓓ

9. When will the budget meeting be held?
    (A) At 10 o'clock today
    (B) Later today
    (C) Sometime tomorrow
    (D) Tomorrow at 10 o'clock   Ⓐ Ⓑ Ⓒ Ⓓ

SHORT TALKS

$\left(\frac{1}{33}\right)$

You will hear short talks given by a single speaker. Listen carefully, and select the best response to each question.

Question 10 refers to the following talk.

10. What is the speaker saying?
    (A) Impressive growth has been achieved.
    (B) Last year's sales are disappointing.
    (C) Sales are on an upward trend.
    (D) Sales haven't changed much recently.   Ⓐ Ⓑ Ⓒ Ⓓ

Questions 11 and 12 refer to the following talk.

11. What is the main topic of the meeting?

    (A) Computer purchases

    (B) How to make meetings shorter

    (C) The budget

    (D) Training   Ⓐ Ⓑ Ⓒ Ⓓ

12. How long are meetings usually?

    (A) About nine hours

    (B) About three hours

    (C) An hour or less

    (D) Any length   Ⓐ Ⓑ Ⓒ Ⓓ

LANGUAGE FOCUS

Pronouns

◎ 次の英文の（　　）内に、最も適当な代名詞を入れてください。

1) I did very little exercise on account of (　　　　　　) injury.
怪我のため私はほとんど運動しなかった。

2) (　　　　　　) serve the best Italian food at that restaurant.
あのレストランでは最高のイタリア料理が出ます。

3) It's always been a dream of (　　　　　) to be on TV.
テレビに出るのはいつも私の夢でした。

4) He was beside (　　　　　) with fury.
彼は怒りで我を忘れていた。

5) (　　　　　) depends how you think about it.
それについてあなたがどう考えるか次第です。

6) She hadn't completed payments on the car, so legally it wasn't really
(　　　　　).
彼女は車の支払いを済ませていない。それで法的には本当に彼女のものではない。

7) The dog would never let (　　　　　) be petted when it was eating.
その犬は食事をしている時に決してなでさせようとしない。

INCOMPLETE SENTENCES

A word or phrase is missing in each of the sentences. Select the best answer to complete the sentence.

13. All of _____ need to do our best to win the game.

    (A) our   (B) ours   (C) us   (D) we

14. People who lie to _____ friends cannot be trusted.

    (A) their   (B) theirs   (C) they   (D) those

15. I thought _____ possible to achieve my goal.

    (A) it   (B) my   (C) one   (D) that

16. Columbus is the capital of Ohio and _____ largest city.

    (A) its   (B) it's   (C) that   (D) that's

17. The human brain is more advanced than _____ of the chimpanzee.

    (A) it   (B) one   (C) that   (D) those

18. He couldn't make _____ understood in English.

    (A) him   (B) his   (C) himself   (D) it

19. He takes _____ for granted that he will follow the path his parents set for him.

    (A) him   (B) his   (C) it   (D) that

20. I'd like to borrow a pencil if you have _____.

    (A) it   (B) mine   (C) one   (D) the one

21. Two of our many members approved the proposal, but _____ didn't.

    (A) other   (B) others   (C) the other   (D) the others

22. Can I have some more milk, if there is _____ left?

    (A) any   (B) it   (C) many   (D) one

23. _____ is set up and I'm ready to roll.

    (A) Anything   (B) Everything   (C) Nothing   (D) Some things

TEXT COMPLETION

Read the email that follows. A word or phrase is missing in some of the sentences. Select the best answer to complete the text.

Questions 24–26 refer to the following company email.

FROM:	Vice-President, Human Resources
TO:	Department Heads
DATE:	September 4th, 20___
SUBJECT:	Reminder: Quarterly review

This email is in connection with the ____ quarterly review meeting. Each
                                        24
department head should read all the attached documents and prepare detailed

data on their performance this quarter ____ summary data for the last year.
                                        25
Please be ready to answer questions on these data. It is ____ that we reach a
                                                            26
decision on the proposals to reduce the number of stores, so be sure to clarify

your own views on the proposals to ensure a fruitful discussion.

<Attached Documents>

---

24. (A) near   (B) next quarter   (C) soon   (D) upcoming

25. (A) as well as   (B) in addition   (C) in conclusion   (D) regarding to

26. (A) crucial   (B) evident   (C) necessitate   (D) significant

Read the text that follows. Select the best answer for each question and mark the letter (A), (B), (C), or (D).

Questions 27–30 refer to the following article.

Ask any employee of most companies what they like least about their job and meetings will almost certainly be one of the answers they give. (Another likely one is email.) Some companies worry about the negative effects of excessive meetings and are taking action to reduce the time lost to them.

One of the most striking of these actions is to install a large clock in the meeting room set to count down to zero from 60 minutes, or whatever the planned meeting length is. This makes people aware of the importance of time and helps to ensure that people do not extend discussion on any topic beyond reasonable limits. Related to this, many companies now set much shorter default times for meetings, such as 30 or 40 minutes. They also require the people who call meetings to send a detailed agenda to all participants in advance, and to set up mailing list or bulletin board discussions on some of the topics, so that the meeting can be used just to make the final decision rather than going through all the arguments.

Meetings are of course useful in making all members of a team feel involved and in getting buy-in from everyone on important decisions. The problem is that companies these days have so many things on which they need to reach decisions, and so many people that the decisions might affect, that it is all too easy to spend hours and hours every day in meetings. High-achievers may get frustrated at all the time they waste in meetings and go somewhere else where their time is valued more highly. At some point, people need to realize that meetings in themselves do not earn the company any money, and take steps to make enough time for more important aspects of their jobs, such as visiting clients and working on already-existing projects.

---

27. Where would this article most likely appear?

    (A) In a business magazine

    (B) In a company annual report

    (C) In an email from a company president to employees

    (D) On a company website

28. Which of the following is NOT mentioned as a way to reduce time spent in meetings?

    (A) Discussing some topics in advance

    (B) Installing a countdown clock

    (C) Planning shorter meetings

    (D) Requiring all participants to help plan the agenda

29. The word "buy-in" in paragraph 3 is closest in meaning to

    (A) a willingness to contribute a small sum of money

    (B) agreement

    (C) discernment

    (D) sales growth

30. In what way are frequent meetings a particular problem with regards to high-achievers?

    (A) They may change jobs.

    (B) They may forget the time or place of a meeting.

    (C) They may not be able to reach a good decision.

    (D) They may not have time to attend some meetings.

COMMUNICATIONS

WARM-UP Ⓐ

Match the words with their correct definitions.

(1) acknowledgment ( )	(a) a change from one state to another
(2) apologize ( )	(b) a place where food is prepared
(3) approve ( )	(c) a sign that you have received something
(4) immediately ( )	(d) a tool
(5) kitchen ( )	(e) right away
(6) participant ( )	(f) someone who takes part in something
(7) spam ( )	(g) the period of time during which most people work
(8) transition ( )	(h) to express a positive view of something
(9) utensil ( )	(i) to say sorry
(10) workday ( )	(j) unwanted email

WARM-UP Ⓑ

Have the following conversation with a partner, filling in the blanks from the box below. Then listen to the recording to check your answers and intonation.

A: We need to _____ this document to the travel _____.

B: Fax? Why?

A: I'm not _____. But some businesses _____ faxes for important documents.

B: Maybe they're considered more _____ than email?

A: I guess _____. Anyway, let's ask _____ we can use the machine in the departmental office.

agency	fax	if	require	secure	so	sure

You will hear four short statements. Look at the picture and choose the statement that best describes what you see.

1.

Ⓐ Ⓑ Ⓒ Ⓓ

2.

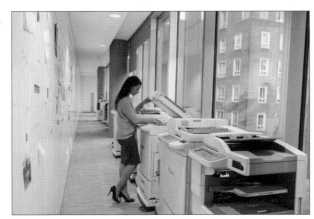

Ⓐ Ⓑ Ⓒ Ⓓ

PART 2 **QUESTION–RESPONSE**

You will hear a question or statement and three responses. Listen carefully, and choose the response to the question or statement.

3. Mark your answer. Ⓐ Ⓑ Ⓒ

4. Mark your answer. Ⓐ Ⓑ Ⓒ

5. Mark your answer. Ⓐ Ⓑ Ⓒ

6. Mark your answer. Ⓐ Ⓑ Ⓒ

SHORT CONVERSATIONS $\left(\frac{1}{36}\right)$

You will hear a short conversation between two or more people. Listen carefully, and select the best response to each question.

Questions 7 through 9 refer to the following conversation.

7.   What has most likely arrived recently?

   (A) A fax from Japan
   (B) A letter from Boston
   (C) A plane from Beijing
   (D) An email from China   Ⓐ Ⓑ Ⓒ Ⓓ

8.   What possible problem is mentioned?

   (A) A misunderstanding
   (B) The weather in Beijing
   (C) The weather in New York
   (D) Transport between Beijing and New York   Ⓐ Ⓑ Ⓒ Ⓓ

9.   What will be done?

   (A) The president will apologize and visit Beijing soon.
   (B) They will avoid any contact with Triple Happiness.
   (C) They will invite the president of Triple Happiness to New York.
   (D) They will invite the president of Triple Happiness to Boston.   Ⓐ Ⓑ Ⓒ Ⓓ

PART 4 **SHORT TALKS** $\left(\frac{1}{37}\right)$

You will hear short talks given by a single speaker. Listen carefully, and select the best response to each question.

Questions 10 through 12 refer to the following announcement.

10. When will the company move to the new intranet system?

   (A) In August
   (B) In July
   (C) When most people in the company agree to cooperate
   (D) When the email problems have been solved

11. What is the biggest problem with the current system?

   (A) People not expressing their meaning clearly
   (B) People sending email to too many people at the same time
   (C) People wasting time writing too many messages
   (D) Spam mail   Ⓐ Ⓑ Ⓒ Ⓓ

12. What is an advantage of AlTogether 3-2-1?

   (A) It has more functions than AlTogether 1-2-3.
   (B) The developers include training in the price of the software.
   (C) It has a good discussion system.
   (D) It has weekly updates.   Ⓐ Ⓑ Ⓒ Ⓓ

LANGUAGE FOCUS

Prepositions

◎ 次の英文を読んで、前置詞がどこに置かれているかを確認してください。

1) I've been wanting to see you **for** ages.
   あなたにずっと会いたいと思っています。

2) They will be here **by** six **in** the morning.
   彼らは午前6時までにここに来ます。

3) The issues are still **under** consideration.
   これらの問題はまだ検討中です。

4) Thanks **to** your help, I was able to graduate **from** this university.
   あなたのおかげで、私はこの大学を卒業できた。

5) We look **upon** him **as** a promising player.
   私たちは彼を前途有望な選手と考えます。

6) Would you lend me something to write **with**?
   何か書くものを貸してもらえませんか？

7) Who are you going to the concert **with**?
   誰と一緒にコンサートに行きますか。

INCOMPLETE SENTENCES

A word or phrase is missing in each of the sentences. Select the best answer to complete the sentence.

13. I saw him _____ the night of October 21.
    (A) at   (B) for   (C) in   (D) on

14. It's nice to be with family and friends _____ Christmas.
    (A) among   (B) at   (C) in   (D) upon

15. We'll ship those items _____ a few hours.
    (A) by   (B) for   (C) in   (D) until

16. I will return the book _____ 3 o'clock.
    (A) during   (B) by   (C) until   (D) while

17. I usually watch the evening news _____ TV at 10.
    (A) by   (B) in   (C) on   (D) over

18. We are _____ children not reading these days.
    (A) worried about   (B) worried at   (C) worry   (D) worrying for

19. The company's offices are located _____ the country.
    (A) among   (B) everywhere   (C) into   (D) throughout

20. Students should avoid walking _____ the woods on their way to school.
    (A) among   (B) between   (C) through   (D) under

21. Be sure to hand your completed report in _____ the end of the day.
    (A) by   (B) through   (C) until   (D) while

22. He wrote a paper for his MBA _____ the economic effects of international trade.
    (A) for   (B) concerned   (C) on   (D) regards

23. Please wait here _____ I come back.
    (A) by   (B) during   (C) until   (D) while

Read the text that follows. A word or phrase is missing in some of the sentences. Select the best answer to complete the text.

Questions 24–26 refer to the following notice.

Any employee using one of the fax machines is ____ to write down on one
                                                        24
of the forms provided by the machines their name and department, and the

destination (company name and fax number) of the fax. The purpose of this

      is to keep track of communications expenses and make sure they are
25
billed to the appropriate department. In addition, we want to review the

trends in fax machine use and see whether it might be possible to reduce the

number of machines or ____ to switch to an electronic method in future.
                        26

24. (A) necessitated   (B) needing   (C) pleaded   (D) requested

25. (A) dilemma   (B) institution   (C) measure   (D) paradox

26. (A) even   (B) eventuality   (C) namely   (D) overtly

Read the texts that follow. Select the best answer for each question.

Questions 27 through 28 refer to the following company announcement.

Communications can be a problem in any organization. As the organization gets bigger, the likelihood of problems increases. For a multinational, multicultural company such as ours, all manner of problems can occur, so it is important that all concerned be aware of the possibilities of misunderstandings, take measures to reduce those possibilities, and have strategies to solve any problems that do occur. The purpose of this document is to give new employees some basic information on this issue as well as steps you can take to further your understanding.

The thousands of employees in our company come from more than 100 countries and speak an astounding twenty-one different mother tongues. All employees are required to get a good score (at least 650) in the TOEIC® or a similar proficiency exam, but that does not mean that they have a native command of the language. Native English speakers are requested to speak reasonably slowly and clearly and avoid using country-specific colloquialisms when communicating with other members of the company.

---

27. What is the purpose of this document?
    (A) To prepare people for a university course on multiculturalism
    (B) To prepare people in a specific company to work better with colleagues from other countries
    (C) To teach people looking for a job about multicultural companies
    (D) To teach young people leaving school about how to do well in a multicultural society

28. How many mother tongues do the employees of the company have?
    (A) 100
    (B) 21
    (C) 650
    (D) Thousands

Questions 29 through 30 refer to the following email.

FROM: Maintenance
TO: All Employees
DATE: September 22nd, 20 ____

Dear all,

We've recently noticed more and more cases of photocopiers being found in an unusable state. As you know, photocopiers are prone to a number of issues, from simple ones like paper jams and toner running out to more difficult ones like lines on paper, ink smudges, and discoloring. Because Maintenance is a small section, we are unable to patrol the whole building looking for problems; we depend on all employees to let us know when there are problems so that we can get to work right away diagnosing the problem and then fixing it, or in some cases calling the supplier (which of course takes extra time). Each photocopier has our extension number. We ask that you call us right away when you come across a malfunctioning machine.

Sincerely,
Fred Willis
Head of Maintenance

29. What problem does Fred Willis refer to?

(A) Some employees have been deliberately damaging the photocopiers.
(B) Some people have not been reporting problems with photocopiers.
(C) Some photocopiers have gone missing.
(D) The company's photocopiers are too old and need replacing.

30. Which of the following statements is true?

(A) Fred Willis has recently retired.
(B) The company contacts the supplier to fix all photocopier problems.
(C) The Maintenance section of the company is very large.
(D) Toner running out is a simple problem that sometimes occurs with photocopiers.

UNIT 10 ADVERTIZING

WARM-UP A

Match the words with their correct definitions.

(1) affordable ( )   (a) a company that operates flights
(2) airline ( )   (b) a place you want to go
(3) baggage ( )   (c) a section of an airport
(4) comprehensive ( )   (d) a senior executive
(5) destination ( )   (e) an electronic device that is often lighter than a laptop
(6) park ( )   (f) done regularly
(7) routine (adj.) ( )   (g) including everything
(8) tablet ( )   (h) not too expensive
(9) terminal ( )   (i) suitcases and bags
(10) vice-president ( )   (j) to leave a car or other vehicle

WARM-UP B

Have the following conversation with a partner, filling in the blanks from the box below. Then listen to the recording to check your answers and intonation.

A: So _____ do you think of these packages I've introduced?

B: They _____ good. Our advertizing _____ isn't very big, so I think we'll go with the Elements package for now.

A: Great. Well, I'll draw up an _____ for you. If you approve it, I'll _____ to work right away.

B: Cool. _____ do you think the estimate will be ready?

A: By tomorrow. Thank you for your _____ today.

B: Thanks for coming. I look forward to hearing from you.

| budget | estimate | get | sound | time | what | when |

PHOTOGRAPHS

You will hear four short statements. Look at the picture and choose the statement that best describes what you see.

1.  Ⓐ Ⓑ Ⓒ Ⓓ

2.  Ⓐ Ⓑ Ⓒ Ⓓ

PART 2

QUESTION-RESPONSE

You will hear a question or statement and three responses. Listen carefully, and choose the response to the question or statement.

3. Mark your answer.   Ⓐ Ⓑ Ⓒ

4. Mark your answer.   Ⓐ Ⓑ Ⓒ

5. Mark your answer.   Ⓐ Ⓑ Ⓒ

6. Mark your answer.   Ⓐ Ⓑ Ⓒ

You will hear short conversations between two or more people. Listen carefully, and select the best response to each question.

Questions 7 through 9 refer to the following conversation.

7. Who telephoned?
    (A) The president of the company
    (B) The sales manager
    (C) The vice-president of human resources
    (D) The vice-president of sales   (A) (B) (C) (D)

8. What kinds of changes are called for?
    (A) Fewer slides
    (B) Less impact
    (C) More detailed explanations
    (D) The use of fewer colors   (A) (B) (C) (D)

9. When is the presentation scheduled to take place?
    (A) Friday afternoon
    (B) Friday morning
    (C) Thursday afternoon
    (D) Thursday evening   (A) (B) (C) (D)

You will hear a short talk given by a single speaker. Listen carefully, and select the best response to each question.

Questions 10 through 12 refer to the following advertisement.

10. According to the advertisement, why is driving yourself to the airport not a good idea?
    (A) Parking at the airport is difficult.
    (B) There is no medical treatment available.
    (C) There is no one to help with baggage.
    (D) You need to go downtown.   (A) (B) (C) (D)

11. How often does the bus go?

    (A) Every 25 minutes
    (B) Every 30 minutes
    (C) Every 45 minutes
    (D) Every hour   Ⓐ Ⓑ Ⓒ Ⓓ

12. Where does the bus terminate?

    (A) At Domestic Terminal 1
    (B) At Domestic Terminal 2
    (C) At International Terminal
    (D) On Eastern Highway   Ⓐ Ⓑ Ⓒ Ⓓ

╭─ LANGUAGE FOCUS ─╮

Relative Clauses

◎ 次の英文を読んで、関係代名詞と関係副詞が文中でどのような役割をしているか確認しましょう。

1) Any politician **who** says such a thing can't be trusted.
   そんなことを言うような政治家は信用できない。

2) This is the office **that** he works in.
   これは彼が働くオフィスです。

3) There were some words **whose** meaning I did not know.
   私には意味が分からない単語がいくつかありました。

4) I have two daughters, **who** are studying at a university in Tokyo.
   私には娘が二人いて、東京の大学で勉強しています。

5) There are some cases in **which** this rule does not apply.
   この規則が適用されない場合がある。

6) The day will come **when** you will have to make a decision by yourself.
   自ら決断しなければならない時が来るだろう。

7) They might be **what** we call gaming addicts.
   彼らはいわゆるゲーム依存症かもしれない。

INCOMPLETE SENTENCES

A word or phrase is missing in each of the sentences. Select the best answer to complete the sentence.

13. The man _____ is standing in front of the bank is my father.

    (A) how   (B) what   (C) which   (D) who

14. Aren't you feeling well? I have a friend _____ is a doctor.

    (A) his husband   (B) the husband of which   (C) of which the husband
    (D) whose husband

15. Sapporo is the city _____ I told you about yesterday.

    (A) that   (B) there   (C) where   (D) what

16. I tried to solve the problem, _____ I found impossible.

    (A) and   (B) it   (C) that   (D) which

17. In the cellar, he found a chest _____ there were many old photographs from his childhood.

    (A) in where   (B) in which   (C) in whose   (D) which

18. His arrival may be delayed, _____ be sure to call me.

    (A) such case   (B) such cases   (C) in there case   (D) in which case

19. In this business, there are times when we have to follow rules _____ we disapprove.

    (A) of which   (B) to what   (C) that   (D) which

20. The influx of people from all over the world to the United States resulted in _____ the melting pot.

    (A) that   (B) that is called   (C) what   (D) what is called

21. I believe that in my lifetime the day will come _____ we can travel around the world in an hour.

    (A) when   (B) whereas   (C) which   (D) while

22. QR codes originated in Japan, _____ more than 5 million users have adopted the technology.

    (A) that   (B) there   (C) where   (D) which

23. I really like sweets. That's _____ it is hard for me to lose weight.

    (A) when   (B) where   (C) which   (D) why

Read the text that follows. A word or phrase is missing in some of the sentences. Select the best answer to complete the text.

Avoiding routine dental work because your insurance doesn't ____ it?
                                                                24

Consider Sunflower Insurance. We believe everyone has a right to affordable,

comprehensive medical care—and that includes dental care. Above all, it

includes regular check-ups and cleanings that help ____ minor problems
                                                    25

developing into major ones that can cost a small fortune to repair. Pay a visit to

our website to find out more. Just input your age, gender, locality, and current

medical conditions to get an estimate of what a year's insurance is likely to ____
                                                                            26

you.

---

24. (A) conceal   (B) cover   (C) do   (D) make

25. (A) preclude   (B) prevent   (C) promote   (D) protect

26. (A) cost   (B) expend   (C) expense   (D) price

Read the text that follows. Select the best answer for each question.

Questions 27–30 refer to the following text.

Eurasian Airlines

Low summer fares to select major destinations. Lock these prices* in by reserving before March 31!

Flights from Tokyo (Kansai**) to:

Athens	$1300 ($1220)
Rome	$1400
Amsterdam	$920 ($1040)
Madrid	$1200 ($1250)
Paris	$1300 ($1300)
London (Heathrow)	$1300 ($1350)
London (Gatwick)	$1250
Frankfurt	$1350
Hong Kong	$720 ($720)
Beijing	$840
Bangkok (Suvarnabhumi)	$855 ($870)
Manila	$900

* All major currencies accepted. Prices listed are for one economy round-trip ticket.
** Available where shown in parentheses.

These fares apply to trips taken between August 1 and September 30. Note that we have competitive fares all year round; please check our website or inquire at one of our offices.

Discount tickets are subject to a cancellation fee of 50% of the cost of the ticket immediately after purchase, and that increases to 80% one week before departure. Sale does not apply to first-class or business tickets. Tickets can be upgraded to Economy Plus for a surcharge of $50 per one-way flight. Complimentary water and light refreshments available on all flights. Full meals must be booked and paid for at least 48 hours in advance, $50 per meal. NOTE: Our offices are closed July 29–31.

27. When would one need to fly to get these discount prices?

    (A) Anytime after March 1st
    (B) Anytime in August or September
    (C) Anytime year round
    (D) Between July 29th and September 30th

28. How much would it cost to buy two Economy Plus round-trip tickets from Kansai to Madrid?

    (A) $2500
    (B) $2600
    (C) $2700
    (D) Those tickets are not available.

29. To which destination is it cheaper to fly from Kansai than from Tokyo?

    (A) Athens
    (B) Bangkok
    (C) London
    (D) It is always cheaper to fly from Tokyo.

30. You bought an economy round-trip ticket from Tokyo to London (Heathrow), with your departure scheduled for August 1st. On June 28th, you cancel your trip. How much money will Eurasian Airlines refund you?

    (A) $260
    (B) $650
    (C) $675
    (D) You are not entitled to a refund.

WARM-UP Ⓐ

Match the words with their correct definitions.

(1)	adaptation	( )	(a) a part of a city far from the downtown area
(2)	applause	( )	(b) an alternative version of a play or novel, etc.
(3)	compose	( )	(c) an elevated platform, often used for performances
(4)	critic	( )	(d) cheap
(5)	crowded	( )	(e) clapping and cheering
(6)	inexpensive	( )	(f) someone who writes reviews of movies, plays, novels, etc.
(7)	popularity	( )	(g) to create a piece of music
(8)	prefer	( )	(h) to like something more than something else
(9)	stage	( )	(i) the degree to which something is liked by many people
(10)	suburb	( )	(j) with lots of people

WARM-UP Ⓑ

Have the following conversation with a partner, filling in the blanks from the box below. Then listen to the recording to check your answers and intonation.

A: Hey, did you _____? Spatz are starting an all-Japan _____ soon.

B: Really? No, I hadn't _____ that. Are they doing a gig here?

A: Yes, on October 21st. I _____ the tickets will disappear pretty soon.

B: Are they already _____ sale?

A: No, they _____ on sale next Wednesday. Shall I _____ tickets for both of us?

book	go	guess	hear	heard	on	tour

You will hear four short statements. Look at the picture and choose the statement that best describes what you see.

1.    Ⓐ Ⓑ Ⓒ Ⓓ

2.    Ⓐ Ⓑ Ⓒ Ⓓ

| PART 2 | **QUESTION-RESPONSE** | $\frac{1}{43}$ |

You will hear a question or statement and three responses. Listen carefully, and choose the response to the question or statement.

3. Mark your answer. Ⓐ Ⓑ Ⓒ

4. Mark your answer. Ⓐ Ⓑ Ⓒ

5. Mark your answer. Ⓐ Ⓑ Ⓒ

6. Mark your answer. Ⓐ Ⓑ Ⓒ

You will hear short conversations between two people. Listen carefully, and select the best response to each question.

Question 7 refers to the following conversation.

7. What are the speakers discussing?

    (A) Their families
    (B) What movies are playing in theaters
    (C) What they will do on the weekend
    (D) Whether they should move house   Ⓐ Ⓑ Ⓒ Ⓓ

Questions 8 through 9 refer to the following conversation.

8. What did the two people do last night?

    (A) They watched a video.
    (B) They went to a movie theater.
    (C) They went to see a play.
    (D) They went to see a soccer match.   Ⓐ Ⓑ Ⓒ Ⓓ

9. Which of the following is true?

    (A) Both of them enjoyed it equally.
    (B) Neither of them enjoyed it.
    (C) The man enjoyed it more than the woman did.
    (D) The woman enjoyed it more than the man did.   Ⓐ Ⓑ Ⓒ Ⓓ

PART 4   **SHORT TALKS**

You will hear short talks given by a single speaker. Listen carefully, and select the best response to each question.

Question 10 refers to the following talk.

10. What is the man talking about?

    (A) A movie theater in his city
    (B) Action movies
    (C) His favorite cities
    (D) The loss of good facilities in city centers   Ⓐ Ⓑ Ⓒ Ⓓ

Questions 11 through 12 refer to the following announcement.

11. What play or plays will be performed at the Festival Theater in the spring?
    (A) A selection of Shakespeare tragedies
    (B) King Lear
    (C) Othello
    (D) Macbeth

    Ⓐ Ⓑ Ⓒ Ⓓ

12. How is the play different from the traditional one?
    (A) It is set in the 20th century.
    (B) It is set in the Middle Ages.
    (C) It is set in England.
    (D) There will be lots of action.

    Ⓐ Ⓑ Ⓒ Ⓓ

⌐ LANGUAGE FOCUS ⌐

Conjunctions

◎ 次の英文の（　　）内から最も適当な接続詞を選んでください。

1) Don't go out in the train without an umbrella, (and, but, or, so)
   you'll catch cold.
   雨の中を傘を持たずに外出しないでください。そうしないと風邪を引きますよ。

2) They got there (if, since, unless, while) it was still dark.
   まだ暗いうちに彼らはそこに着いた。

3) My mother stayed in the room (by, for, since, until) her baby fell
   asleep.
   私の母は赤ん坊が寝入るまで部屋にいた。

4) She does not like vegetables, (and, but, nor, so) does she like meat.
   彼女は野菜が好きではないし、それに肉も好きではない。

5) It's a bit cool (in order that, not that, now that, so that) the sun's set.
   日が暮れたので少し涼しい。

6) You should leave now (as soon as, in case, in order that, whenever)
   traffic is heavy.
   交通渋滞があると行けないのでもう出発したほうが良いです。

7) (Encountering, Due to, In case of, If encountered) emergency, press
   the button and speak into the speakerphone.
   緊急の場合には、ボタンを押して、スピーカーホンに話しかけてください。

INCOMPLETE SENTENCES

A word or phrase is missing in each of the sentences. Select the best answer to complete the sentence.

13. I went home early _____ I was injured in the match.

    (A) although   (B) because   (C) having   (D) so

14. _____ I face a problem, I always contact the help desk.

    (A) Every   (B) If that   (C) When that   (D) Whenever

15. I haven't seen that report _____ the first draft was circulated more than a month ago.

    (A) because   (B) since   (C) whereas   (D) while

16. _____ you get a car, you can go anywhere you want.

    (A) Once   (B) So   (C) Till   (D) While

17. _____ you have a better idea, why don't we try out what John suggested just now?

    (A) If   (B) Lest   (C) Unless   (D) Whereas

18. The journey takes nearly an hour _____ the bus stops at every bus stop.

    A) also   (B) as   (C) or   (D) which

19. Being a successful student requires not only hard work _____ clarity of purpose.

    (A) but also   (B) but never   (C) or   (D) without

20. Get up early, _____ you will be late for school.

    (A) and   (B) but   (C) for   (D) or

21. _____ that our children have grown up, we travel more often than before.

    (A) Now   (B) Since   (C) Therefore   (D) Then

22. Antarctica is dry, cold, and windy, _____ penguins and a few other animal species live there.

    (A) notwithstanding   (B) or   (C) therefore   (D) yet

23. You can come along to the meeting _____ you don't say anything.

    (A) as long as   (B) or   (C) providing for   (D) so long

TEXT COMPLETION

Read the text that follows. A word or phrase is missing in some of the sentences. Select the best answer to complete the text.

Questions 24–26 refer to the following announcement.

Star Multiplex

Residents will be delighted to hear that a new Star Multiplex will be opening in December. These days, with the rising popularity of on-demand video and home theater systems, more and more people are staying at home to watch movies.

But nothing compares to seeing a movie where it is meant to ____ —on the big
24
screen! Unfortunately, in recent years theaters have moved to the suburbs and prices have gone up, meaning that young people without their own cars have had difficulty getting to the theater.

That ends now. We think movie theaters belong in the city center, so ____ we're
25
building one. Star Multiplex will have 14 screens including an IMAX screen! In addition to theaters, it will also have a bowling alley and an amusement center.

You will be able to see movies in the city center, where you like to do your shopping, near Stadler Department Store and your other favorite shops.

Remember: it's coming in December. We ____ seeing you there.
26

---

24. (A) be seeing   (B) be seen   (C) see   (D) seeing

25. (A) here is   (B) resultant   (C) that is   (D) that's where

26. (A) are looking   (B) enjoy   (C) look forward to   (D) looking to

READING COMPREHENSION

Read the text and select the best answer for each question.

Questions 27–30 refer to the following text message chain.

Jason Smith:
Hey, are you free on Sunday?

Tim Clinton:
Sure, what do you have in mind?

Jason Smith:
Thinking of going to see the new Star Adventure film.

Tim Clinton:
Oh, didn't realize it was coming out so soon. Sounds good. Let's do it!

Jason Smith:
The evening screenings will probably be pretty crowded. Let's go to an early one.

Tim Clinton:
Sure. Do you know the schedule?

Jason Smith:
Yes, there's a screening at 9:30.

Tim Clinton:
Are you talking about Sunstar Cinemas or the Piccadilly?

Jason Smith:
The latter.

Tim Clinton:
Cool. Let's go to that screening. We should probably get there early.

Jason Smith:
Yeah, how about meeting in front of the cinema at 9:15?

Tim Clinton:
Could do that. Or we could meet a bit earlier and have breakfast first.

Jason Smith:
That's an idea. OK, how about meeting at Norton's Coffee at 8:45? They've got good pancakes and it's pretty inexpensive.

Tim Clinton:
Might be better to make it 8:30. Don't want to be late for the film.

Jason Smith:
Sounds like a plan.

27. What does Tim Clinton mean when he says: "didn't realize it was coming out so soon"?

    (A) He thought the first screening would be later in the day.

    (B) He does not want to go out so early in the morning.

    (C) He thought the release date of the movie was later in the year.

    (D) He wishes that Jason Smith had not woken him up.

28. Which movie theater will they go to?

    (A) Norton's Cinema

    (B) The Piccadilly

    (C) Sunstar Cinemas

    (D) They will decide later.

29. Where and when will they meet?

    (A) At Norton's Coffee at 8:30

    (B) At Norton's Coffee at 8:45

    (C) At Norton's Coffee at 9:15

    (D) In front of the movie theater at 9:15

30. What does Jason Smith mean when he says: "Sounds like a plan"?

    (A) He agrees with Tim's idea of meeting earlier.

    (B) He believes Tim will become a good planner after he leaves school.

    (C) He doesn't want to go to the movie theater.

    (D) He likes the pronunciation of the word "plan".

WARM-UP Ⓐ

Match the words with their correct definitions.

(1) client   (   )

(2) frequent   (   )

(3) interact   (   )

(4) interview   (   )

(5) promotion   (   )

(6) proposal   (   )

(7) report   (   )

(8) requirement   (   )

(9) résumé   (   )

(10) word processing (   )

(a) a conversation used to determine someone's suitability for a job

(b) a document that gives some ideas for evaluation

(c) a document that summarizes one's education and work experience

(d) a document that summarizes work done or a situation

(e) a kind of customer

(f) happening often

(g) moving to a higher position in a company

(h) something that is necessary for a job, for example

(i) the creation and editing of text documents on a computer

(j) to talk with other people

WARM-UP Ⓑ

Have the following conversation with a partner, filling in the blanks from the box below. Then listen to the recording to check your answers and intonation.

A: Could you tell me a _____ about your work _____ up until now?

B: Sure. I had some _____ jobs as a student, but I have only had one _____ job.

A: The _____ at Smiths, Inc?

B: That's _____. I was there for five years.

A: Was that a _____ experience for you?

B: Not at all, it was great. But I need a new challenge.

bit	experience	full-time	negative	one	part-time	right

You will hear four short statements. Look at the picture and choose the statement that best describes what you see.

1.

Ⓐ Ⓑ Ⓒ Ⓓ

2.

Ⓐ Ⓑ Ⓒ Ⓓ

PART 2   **QUESTION–RESPONSE** $\left(\frac{1}{48}\right)$

You will hear a question or statement and three responses. Listen carefully, and choose the response to the question or statement.

3. Mark your answer.   Ⓐ Ⓑ Ⓒ

4. Mark your answer.   Ⓐ Ⓑ Ⓒ

5. Mark your answer.   Ⓐ Ⓑ Ⓒ

6. Mark your answer.   Ⓐ Ⓑ Ⓒ

You will hear short conversations between two or more people. Listen carefully, and select the best response to each question.

Questions 7 through 9 refer to the following conversation.

7. What kind of job does this conversation concern?
   (A) A computer programmer
   (B) A researcher
   (C) A salesperson
   (D) A website developer   (A) (B) (C) (D)

8. What kind of software expertise is NOT required?
   (A) creating presentations
   (B) database management
   (C) making websites
   (D) word processing   (A) (B) (C) (D)

9. What is the situation at the end of the conversation?
   (A) The man has been offered a job and has decided to accept it.
   (B) The man has decided not to work for the woman's company.
   (C) The man is considering whether to accept an offer from the woman.
   (D) The woman is considering whether to offer the job to the man.
      (A) (B) (C) (D)

PART 4   **SHORT TALKS**

You will hear short talks given by a single speaker. Listen carefully, and select the best response to each question.

Questions 10 through 12 refer to the following announcement.

10. What is going to happen over the next week in the company?
    (A) Changes in senior positions
    (B) Meetings of certain employees with the company's president
    (C) Performance reviews for all staff
    (D) The annual drama performances   (A) (B) (C) (D)

11. What is the purpose of the reviews?

    (A) To discipline workers who have performed badly

    (B) To discuss ways to make employees' work more effective and to give them better support

    (C) To give guidance to workers who are being fired

    (D) To identify workers whose salaries should be decreased   Ⓐ Ⓑ Ⓒ Ⓓ

12. Who will most employees meet with?

    (A) An outside consultant

    (B) The director of their division

    (C) The president of the company

    (D) Their immediate supervisor   Ⓐ Ⓑ Ⓒ Ⓓ

LANGUAGE FOCUS

Quantifiers

◎ 次の英文の（　　）内から、最も適当な語句を選んでください。

1) Can I have (a, another, any, some) more coffee, please?
コーヒーのお代わりをください。

2) She watches a lot of movies, but I don't watch (many, much, little, less).
彼女は映画をたくさん観るが、私はあまり観ない。

3) He was (most of, none of, not a little) disappointed when he heard the news.
彼はその知らせを聞いて少なからず落胆した。

4) (All, Much, None) of a sudden, the lights went out.
突然、明かりが消えた。

5) (All, Each, Every) of us is a fan of the group.
私たちは皆、そのグループのファンだ。

6) I have two daughters; one is in Tokyo, and (another, other, the other) in Sapporo.
私には二人の娘がいて、一人は東京、もう一人は札幌にいる。

7) I've decided to learn English for (a number, the number, many, some) of reasons.
いくつかの理由から英語を学ぶことを決めました。

A word or phrase is missing in each of the sentences. Select the best answer to complete the sentence.

13. I'm looking for _____ paper for the photocopier.

    (A) a   (B) any   (C) one   (D) some

14. We had very _____ snow last winter.

    (A) few   (B) little   (C) many   (D) several

15. Innovation is key to success in _____ industries.

    (A) anything   (B) many   (C) much   (D) none

16. The doctor told him that it's important for him to do _____ exercise every day.

    (A) a few   (B) a little   (C) any   (D) many

17. She found _____ grammatical errors when she checked my work.

    (A) any   (B) quite a few   (C) quite a little   (D) quite a lot

18. _____ is known about her plans.

    (A) A few   (B) Few   (C) Lest   (D) Very little

19. _____ cats have been living on campus since I don't know when.

    (A) Any   (B) Each   (C) Every   (D) Several

20. _____ adults need 7 or 8 hours of sleep to feel their best.

    (A) All of   (B) Almost   (C) Most   (D) Mostly

21. The two mountaineers were exhausted but _____ of them was injured.

    (A) either   (B) few   (C) neither   (D) nobody

22. We interviewed fifteen candidates for the position, but _____ of them was suitable.

    (A) few   (B) neither   (C) nobody   (D) none

23. He spends _____ his free time playing basketball.

    (A) a few   (B) almost   (C) most   (D) most of

Read the text that follows. A word or phrase is missing in some of the sentences. Select the best answer to complete the text.

Questions 24–26 refer to the following notice.

A small software company in the Seattle area is looking for software

developers. The company creates and ____ a broad library of web, desktop
                                    24

and mobile applications and is looking for developers with experience in all

these areas. ____ positions require willingness to relocate to Seattle. These
             25

positions feature competitive salary and excellent benefits and opportunities

to travel to conferences. Contract work also available. To apply or inquire,

contact Mr. Lopez at lopez@seattlesoft.com. Those applying should include a

résumé and at least one reference. For ____ details, visit seattlesoft.com.
                                        26

---

24. (A) discards   (B) maintains   (C) perpetuates   (D) perseveres

25. (A) 24/7   (B) All-days   (C) Full-time   (D) Temporary

26. (A) extra   (B) farther   (C) further   (D) supplementary

Read the text that follows. Select the best answer for each question.

Questions 27–30 refer to the following article.

Job Prospects in STEM Subjects

College students in STEM subjects will be pleased to hear that job opportunities are likely to continue to improve over the next several years. More and more jobs require advanced knowledge of science or engineering fields, often with strong math skills, as more and more unskilled or routine jobs are shifted overseas and the engine room of the economy shifts to new technologies. Graduates in these fields are likely to get higher salaries and better job security.

Another positive change is that, while these jobs have until now been dominated by men, a larger and larger proportion of new posts is being filled by women. Companies hiring in these fields tend to be quite modern in approach and generally do not feature old-boy networks, meaning that women are welcome to apply and, if sufficiently skilled, are as likely to be hired as men.

Since the world is unlikely to stop changing once you have found a job, you will find that strong technical skills or knowledge, while important, will not be enough. Employers want evidence of a well-rounded personality and an ability to work as part of a team. They also value "softer" skills such as knowledge of foreign languages, even in the age of computer translation, which are not only valuable in themselves but also provide evidence of general intelligence and a broad willingness to learn.

27. What is the M in STEM most likely to stand for?

   (A) major
   (B) math
   (C) minority
   (D) men

28. What kind of change in the economy does the article refer to?

  (A) Companies are making new kinds of engines.
  (B) Mathematical ability is now essential in all jobs.
  (C) New technologies are becoming more important.
  (D) Skilled jobs are moving overseas.

29. What change in science and engineering jobs is referred to?

  (A) Old-boy networks have become increasingly important.
  (B) There are more opportunities for women than before.
  (C) Women have to be more skilled than men do.
  (D) Women can now get higher salaries than men can.

30. What is said about foreign languages?

  (A) They are no longer useful because translation can be done by computers.
  (B) They are not useful in themselves but show general intelligence.
  (C) They can help people to work in international teams.
  (D) They are valuable.

TRIPS & VACATIONS

WARM-UP (A)

Match the words with their correct definitions.

(1) accommodations ( )
(2) backpack ( )
(3) enriching ( )
(4) precaution ( )
(5) promotion ( )
(6) rail ( )
(7) reservation ( )
(8) story ( )
(9) temple ( )
(10) vaccination ( )

(a) a booking at a hotel, on a transit system, etc.
(b) a kind of bag for storing and carrying things
(c) a level in a building
(d) a place of worship in Buddhism and other religions
(e) a transit system using trains
(f) a way to protect against diseases
(g) fulfilling, valuable
(h) getting a higher position
(i) hotels and other places to stay
(j) something you do to avoid a future problem

WARM-UP (B)

Have the following conversation with a partner, filling in the blanks from the box below. Then listen to the recording to check your answers and intonation.

A: Have you ever been _____?

B: Yes, I _____ Taiwan once on a high school trip. And I went to Korea in the spring vacation in my first year of _____.

A: How _____ Taiwan?

B: I really _____ it. But the trip wasn't long _____. How about you?

A: I've never been _____ Japan but I hope to go somewhere before I graduate.

| abroad | college | enjoyed | enough | outside | visited | was |

PART 1   PHOTOGRAPHS

You will hear four short statements. Look at the picture and choose the statement that best describes what you see.

1.

Ⓐ Ⓑ Ⓒ Ⓓ

2.

Ⓐ Ⓑ Ⓒ Ⓓ

PART 2   QUESTION–RESPONSE

You will hear a question or statement and three responses. Listen carefully, and choose the response to the question or statement.

3. Mark your answer.   Ⓐ Ⓑ Ⓒ

4. Mark your answer.   Ⓐ Ⓑ Ⓒ

5. Mark your answer.   Ⓐ Ⓑ Ⓒ

6. Mark your answer.   Ⓐ Ⓑ Ⓒ

SHORT CONVERSATIONS

You will hear short conversations between two people. Listen carefully, and select the best response to each question.

Question 7 refers to the following conversation.

7. What is the man doing?

    (A) Asking about lost property
    (B) Preparing to go to New Zealand
    (C) Shopping for a backpack
    (D) Waiting for a minute   Ⓐ Ⓑ Ⓒ Ⓓ

Questions 8 through 9 refer to the following conversation.

8. What do the children have planned during the summer?

    (A) A reservation
    (B) A week by the sea
    (C) An economics class
    (D) Summer school and a school trip   Ⓐ Ⓑ Ⓒ Ⓓ

9. What do the parents decide to do in the summer vacation?

    (A) They decide not to go on a family trip.
    (B) They will check how many points the children get at the summer school.
    (C) They will give it to Ms. Kidd.
    (D) They will go to the seaside.   Ⓐ Ⓑ Ⓒ Ⓓ

SHORT TALKS

You will hear short talks given by a single speaker. Listen carefully, and select the best response to each question.

Question 10 refers to the following talk.

10. What is the most popular place to visit in France?

    (A) Paris
    (B) the Loire
    (C) the Mediterranean coast
    (D) the castles   Ⓐ Ⓑ Ⓒ Ⓓ

Question 11 refers to the following announcement.

11. Who is making this announcement?

    (A) a hotel receptionist

    (B) a musician

    (C) a traffic police officer

    (D) a tour guide   (A) (B) (C) (D)

Question 12 refers to the following announcement.

12. How long does it take to fly direct from California to New Zealand?

    (A) the next day

    (B) 12 hours

    (C) 10 hours

    (D) three and a half hours   (A) (B) (C) (D)

LANGUAGE FOCUS

Easily Confused Words

◎ 次の英文の（　　）内から最も適当な語句を選んでください。

1) I suggest you (to try, try, will try) again tomorrow.
   明日もう一度やったらどうですか。

2) We were made (to work, work, working) all night.
   私たちは徹夜させられた。

3) I will lend you my digital camera, (unless, provided, so) that you use it carefully.
   大事に使うのであれば、私のデジタルカメラを貸してあげます。

4) A man is known (by, for, to) the company he keeps.
   人は付き合っている友だちを見れば分かる。

5) Why do you take it for (possibility, granted, accounting) that you will fail?
   なぜ自分が失敗するのが当然だと思いますか。

6) A good teacher (courages, discourages, encourages) students to study harder.
   良い先生は学生たちを勇気づけていっそう勉強させることができる。

7) The employees waited (anxiety, anxiously, anxious) to see the reaction of the CEO to their report.
   従業員たちは自分たちの報告書に対する CEO の反応を心配そうに見守った。

INCOMPLETE SENTENCES

A word or phrase is missing in each of the sentences. Select the best answer to complete the sentence.

13. The typhoon _____ us cancel the trip.

    (A) caused   (B) forced   (C) got   (D) made

14. John is _____ student in this class.

    (A) the second taller   (B) the second tallest   (C) the taller second
    (D) the tallest second

15. Alaska is larger than _____ in the U.S.

    (A) another state   (B) another states   (C) any other state
    (D) any other states

16. You _____ tell this secret to anyone.

    (A) had better not   (B) had better not to   (C) had not better
    (D) had not better to

17. She _____ anything after nine in the evening.

    (A) eats seldom   (B) is seldom eating   (C) seldom eats
    (D) seldom is eating

18. My experiences during my time overseas were _____.

    (A) dear   (B) evaluative   (C) expensive   (D) invaluable

19. It wouldn't be _____ to wear excessively casual clothes to tonight's party.

    (A) appropriate   (B) friendly   (C) insultingly   (D) interesting

20. This ground is half the _____ of that one.

    (A) big   (B) large   (C) size   (D) small

21. The crisis necessitated a _____ overhaul of financial regulations.

    (A) complete   (B) fair   (C) rooted   (D) whole

22. As members of a government organization, we are _____ to the public.

    (A) accountable   (B) accountant   (C) representing   (D) responsing

23. Is there _____ around here we can get something to eat?

    (A) anything   (B) anywhere   (C) many places   (D) something

TEXT COMPLETION

Read the text that follows. A word or phrase is missing in some of the sentences. Select the best answer to complete the text.

Questions 24–26 refer to the following notice.

Traveling can be an enjoyable and enriching experience but it is important

to take the necessary ____ to avoid health problems, which can spoil an
                          24

otherwise fine trip. If you have any pre-existing medical conditions, have a

check-up before you leave, and make sure you have sufficient medications for

your whole trip. ____ advice from your embassy regarding any vaccinations
                   25

that you may need before leaving, and be sure to do that in plenty of time, as

not all vaccinations are immediately available. In addition, many vaccinations

do not ____ immediately, and it may even be necessary to have the same
        26

vaccination twice with a certain number of days or weeks between them.

24. (A) attention   (B) precautions   (C) risks   (D) warnings

25. (A) Check in   (B) Inspect   (C) Look for   (D) Ratify

26. (A) affect   (B) last   (C) make effective   (D) take effect

Read the text that follows. Select the best answer for each question and mark the letter (A), (B), (C), or (D).

Questions 27–30 refer to the following article.

Students and other young people looking for something interesting to do in vacations and a way to gain useful experience—as well as a chance to practice English—should consider a rail trip through Europe, which is made convenient by Eurail Passes.

A Eurail Pass is a special train ticket that can be used in Europe as many times as you like for a certain number of days or weeks. Most students based in Asia used to buy the Select Pass, which was a cost-effective option but required you to choose four neighboring countries in advance, or a Regional Pass. These have been phased out and instead the Global Pass, which allows travel to 33 countries, has been reduced in price. Unless you plan to visit only a single country, in which case a One Country Pass will fit the bill, this is the one you want.

The Eurail Pass itself isn't too expensive, but of course the Pass is not your only expense: you will also need to buy a plane ticket to Europe, and of course you need the money for your accommodations in Europe. To reduce expense, it is best to avoid the summer vacation even though that is the time of year when it is easiest to find the time to go traveling. Flights are much cheaper in the spring vacation, as are accommodations. To further save on accommodations, it is best to look for youth hostels rather than hotels. Another trick is to plan your travels so that you take night trains whenever possible, which also saves you the trouble of finding a place to stay.

---

27. According to the writer of this article, what kind of Eurail Pass is of most interest to students from Asia?
    (A) The Global Pass
    (B) The Select Pass
    (C) The One Country Pass
    (D) The Regional Pass

28. What is a Eurail Global Pass?
    (A) A special ticket that allows you to travel by rail in many countries in Europe
    (B) A special ticket that allows you to travel on rail systems throughout the world
    (C) A special ticket that allows you to travel on rail and bus systems
    (D) An alternative name for the Select Pass

29. When is the best time for students to travel in Europe?
    (A) Exam time
    (B) The spring vacation
    (C) The summer vacation
    (D) The winter vacation

30. Which of the following is NOT recommended in the passage as a way to save money?
    (A) Buying a Eurail Pass
    (B) Staying at a youth hostel
    (C) Taking a night train
    (D) Traveling in the summer vacation

WARM-UP Ⓐ

Match the words with their correct definitions.

(1) commute	( )	(a)	a measure of temperature
(2) degree	( )	(b)	a scientist who specializes in the weather
(3) forward (v.)	( )	(c)	a strip of land used by airplanes to take off and land
(4) inadequate	( )	(d)	an outbreak of a disease across a wide area and many people
(5) meteorologist	( )	(e)	coming at a fortunate time
(6) pandemic	( )	(f)	not enough
(7) petroleum	( )	(g)	oil
(8) runway	( )	(h)	to send a received email on to a new recipient
(9) timely	( )	(i)	to travel regularly between home and work or school
(10) vulnerable	( )	(j)	weak or unable to respond to attack

WARM-UP Ⓑ

Have the following conversation with a partner, filling in the blanks from the box below. Then listen to the recording to check your answers and intonation.

A: Were you OK in the storms last _____?

B: Well, _____ was some flooding near my house. We weren't able to go _____ for a couple hours.

A: Oh, really? That sounds bad.

B: Well, it's not a _____ now. Were you OK?

A: _____, we have a small leak in our _____.

B: That's _____ bad!

out	problem	roof	there	too	unfortunately	week

You will hear four short statements. Look at the picture and choose the statement that best describes what you see.

1.

(A) (B) (C) (D)

2.

(A) (B) (C) (D)

PART 2 | **QUESTION-RESPONSE**

You will hear a question or statement and three responses. Listen carefully, and choose the response to the question or statement.

3. Mark your answer.

(A) (B) (C)

4. Mark your answer.

(A) (B) (C)

5. Mark your answer.

(A) (B) (C)

6. Mark your answer.

(A) (B) (C)

You will hear short conversations between two or more people. Listen carefully, and select the best response to each question.

Questions 7 through 8 refer to the following conversation.

7. What is the weather like?

   (A) Cold
   (B) Rainy
   (C) Snowy
   (D) Windy   Ⓐ Ⓑ Ⓒ Ⓓ

8. Is the flight going to be canceled?

   (A) No.
   (B) It seems likely.
   (C) It seems unlikely.
   (D) Yes.   Ⓐ Ⓑ Ⓒ Ⓓ

Question 9 refers to the following conversation.

9. What does the man decide to do?

   (A) He hasn't decided yet.
   (B) He will go to work.
   (C) He will stay at home.
   (D) He will telephone his workplace to discuss the situation. Ⓐ Ⓑ Ⓒ Ⓓ

You will hear short talks given by a single speaker. Listen carefully, and select the best response to each question.

Questions 10 through 12 refer to the following announcement.

10. What was the highest temperature in England today?

   (A) 37 degrees
   (B) 38 degrees
   (C) 40 degrees
   (D) 42 degrees   Ⓐ Ⓑ Ⓒ Ⓓ

11. What else is said about today's weather?

    (A) It was windy.

    (B) It was cool in some parts.

    (C) It was cooler than last week.

    (D) There was almost no wind.   Ⓐ Ⓑ Ⓒ Ⓓ

12. Which of the following is NOT said?

    (A) Air conditioning in England tends to be inadequate.

    (B) Temperatures next week are expected to be much cooler.

    (C) There are worries that temperatures may go even higher in the future.

    (D) There were some very hot days last week.   Ⓐ Ⓑ Ⓒ Ⓓ

LANGUAGE FOCUS

More Easily Confused Words

◎ 次の英文の（　　）内から、最も適当な語（句）を選んでください。

1) The branch office in New York will be closed on Friday (at, for, on) a national holiday.
ニューヨークにある支店は国民の祝日のために金曜日に休業します。

2) After many years (of use, used, useful), the washing machine finally stopped working.
長年使っていた洗濯機がとうとう故障した。

3) You'd better make the (many, most, much) of this opportunity.
この機会をうまく生かしなさい。

4) She wrote her master's thesis (among, along, under) the guidance of her academic supervisor.
彼女は指導教授の指導の下で修士論文を作成した。

5) (No one, Nobody, None) of my friends can speak French.
私の友達は誰もフランス語が話せないんです。

6) The company's hiring strategy is quite different from (one, that, those) of its main competitor.
その会社の採用戦略は主な競合社のものとはかなり異なっています。

7) Our employees are encouraged to participate (regular, regularly, regularity) in community programs.
我が社の従業員は地域活動のプログラムに定期的に参加するように推奨されている。

A word or phrase is missing in each of the sentences. Select the best answer to complete the sentence.

13. Everyone was a little worried when the client got up _____ leave.

    (A) as for   (B) for   (C) in order   (D) to

14. He always maintained a cheerful manner _____ his grave illness.

    (A) although   (B) as well as   (C) but for   (D) in spite of

15. _____ enough time and money, I'd take a year or two off work to study for an MBA.

    (A) Given was I   (B) Given were I   (C) Had I   (D) I would have

16. The actor continues to enjoy a successful career _____ his lack of any obvious talent for acting.

    (A) even though   (B) despite   (C) in favor of   (D) in spite

17. He was _____ to believe in hard work and honesty.

    (A) brought up   (B) grown up   (C) raised up   (D) taken up

18. When you look up a word in the dictionary, you should look through all the _____ to make sure you have really understood the meaning.

    (A) defining   (B) definitions   (C) distinctions   (D) meaning

19. An overseas _____ would be a good way for you to get work experience and improve your language skills.

    (A) internship   (B) opportunist   (C) payment   (D) teacher

20. I must have _____ you. I thought you said you were leaving tonight.

    (A) heard   (B) misheard   (C) misunderstanding   (D) uncomprehended

21. At your annual review the directors will criticize your work but you shouldn't _____ it too personally.

    (A) get   (B) have   (C) make   (D) take

22. Our mother is very kind, _____ our father is very strict with us.

    (A) as   (B) during   (C) when   (D) while

23. Marketing is of course essential but quality assurance must always be a _____.

    (A) prior   (B) firstly   (C) priority   (D) firsthand

TEXT COMPLETION

Read the text that follows. A word or phrase is missing in some of the sentences.
Select the best answer to complete the text.

Tropical storm Margaret _____ the Caribbean on Saturday, _____ heavy
                          24   **25**
rain and strong winds. The storm is expected to _____ over the next few
                                                  26
days, so residents should take the greatest care when going outside.

24. (A) came   (B) entered   (C) go through   (D) went

25. (A) bring   (B) bringing   (C) brought   (D) caused

26. (A) be fine   (B) get better   (C) rain   (D) worsen

Questions 27 through 30 refer to the following e-mails. Select the best answer for each question.

TO: Undisclosed recipients
FROM: The Office of Social Resilience, GOV
SUBJECT: Resilience building

Dear Business leader,

Recent years have seen the financial crash, a global pandemic, war, and extreme weather events. —[**1**]— These challenges indicate that we have left the comparatively prosperous and peaceful post-Cold War period behind, and entered a new era of instability and shocks to our economy and society.

As a business leader, you have no doubt had to overcome many challenges to your business during this time. —[**2**]— In a recent review, the government concluded that our country needs a new program of resilience building. Our physical infrastructure is in many places rather old, and our logistical systems depend on smooth global trade that can bring us any goods we need as soon as we need them. Too much of our energy depends on petroleum. This makes us vulnerable to global fluctuations in price. —[**3**]— This means that we use too much energy and it is difficult to prevent the spread of infection during times of epidemics or pandemics.

—[**4**]— To help businesses meet these challenges, the government has set up a number of programs that offer grants and tax breaks. These include:
• Physical Infrastructure Upgrade: This program offers support to businesses and other organizations who improve buildings in ways that increase energy efficiency, improve ventilation, or make them more habitable in extreme hot weather.
• Logistics Upgrade: This program can be used by companies that institute systems for dealing with supply disruptions by increasing stockpiles of key goods or for making it easier for employees to work from home in emergencies, and so on.

You can find more details on these and other programs at our website: https://upgrade.resilience.gov

Sincerely,
Veronica Haaland,
Office of Social Resilience

TO:	Jim Leeson, Greg Emms, Samantha Wang
FROM:	B. Svenson, Clapton Enterprises
SUBJECT:	[FORWARDED:] Resilience grants?

Dear Samantha, Jim, and Greg,

I am forwarding you this email from the government's Office of Social Resilience. Since we have been thinking about having employees split their time between the office and home, this could be timely. The website also mentions the *Quality of Life Upgrade* program, which we might be able to use to get support for upgrading our gym and health benefits for our workers.
How are your schedules tomorrow? If possible, I'd like to get together to get your preliminary thoughts on the feasibility of applying for one or more of these programs.

Best,
Barbara

27. In which position marked [1], [2], [3], and [4] does the following sentence best belong?
    "Our buildings have poor insulation and ventilation."
    (A) [1]   (B) [2]
    (C) [3]   (D) [4]

28. Which office of Social Resilience program is mentioned in the second e-mail but not in the first?
    (A) Logistics Upgrade   (B) Physical Infrastructure Upgrade
    (C) Quality of Life Upgrade   (D) Global Warming Recovery

29. The word "prosperous" in paragraph 1 of the e-mail from Ms. Haaland is closest in meaning to
    (A) perilous   (B) quiet
    (C) stable   (D) wealthy

30. What is the purpose of Ms. Svenson's e-mail?
    (A) To advertize a website
    (B) To try to arrange a meeting
    (C) To encourage employees to work from home more often
    (D) To get a final decision on applying for a government program

PART 1

PART 1 **PHOTOGRAPHS**

You will hear four short statements. Look at the picture and choose the statement that best describes what you see.

1.  Ⓐ Ⓑ Ⓒ Ⓓ

2.  Ⓐ Ⓑ Ⓒ Ⓓ

PART 2 **QUESTION-RESPONSE**

You will hear a question or statement and three responses. Listen carefully, and choose the response to the question or statement.

3. Mark your answer.   Ⓐ Ⓑ Ⓒ

4. Mark your answer.   Ⓐ Ⓑ Ⓒ

5. Mark your answer.   Ⓐ Ⓑ Ⓒ

6. Mark your answer.   Ⓐ Ⓑ Ⓒ

PART 3 **SHORT CONVERSATIONS**

You will hear short conversations between two or more people. Listen carefully, and select the best response to each question.

Question 7 refers to the following conversation.

7. What is the man doing?
   (A) Asking about lost property
   (B) Buying a flag
   (C) Shopping for a backpack
   (D) Waiting for a minute   Ⓐ Ⓑ Ⓒ Ⓓ

Question 8 refers to the following conversation.

8. What does the man decide to do?
   (A) He hasn't decided yet.
   (B) He will go to work.
   (C) He will stay at home.
   (D) He will telephone his workplace to discuss the situation.   Ⓐ Ⓑ Ⓒ Ⓓ

Question 9 refers to the following conversation.

9. What are the two speakers going to do?
   (A) The man doesn't want to go out.
   (B) They're going to a Chinese restaurant.
   (C) They're going to an Italian restaurant.
   (D) They're going to decide later.   Ⓐ Ⓑ Ⓒ Ⓓ

PART 4 SHORT TALKS

You will hear short talks given by a single speaker. Listen carefully, and select the best response to each question.

Question 10 refers to the following talk.

10. When does the speaker go swimming?

   (A) Every day
   (B) Friday
   (C) Monday
   (D) Thursday   Ⓐ Ⓑ Ⓒ Ⓓ

Question 11 refers to the following talk.

11. What kind of restriction is mentioned in the e-mail?

   (A) The drugs that doctors can prescribe
   (B) The length of hospitalization
   (C) The total cost of treatment
   (D) Which hospitals employees can use   Ⓐ Ⓑ Ⓒ Ⓓ

Question 12 refers to the following talk.

12. According to the speaker, which of the following statements is true?

   (A) Eating breakfast is not a good idea.
   (B) It is important to eat breakfast.
   (C) Many people don't like to eat or study.
   (D) You may skip breakfast if you are not hungry.   Ⓐ Ⓑ Ⓒ Ⓓ

PART 5 INCOMPLETE SENTENCES

A word or phrase is missing in each of the sentences. Select the best answer to complete the sentence.

13. He always maintained a cheerful manner _____ his grave illness.
   (A) although   (B) as well as   (C) but for   (D) in spite of

14. My experiences during my time overseas were _____.
   (A) dear   (B) evaluative   (C) expensive   (D) invaluable

15. She found _____ grammatical errors when she checked my work.
   (A) any   (B) quite a few   (C) quite a little   (D) quite a lot

16. _____ I face a problem, I always contact the help desk.
   (A) every   (B) if that   (C) when that   (D) whenever

17. Sapporo is the city _____ I told you about yesterday.
   (A) that   (B) there   (C) where   (D) whereof

18. Please wait here _____ I come back.

(A) by   (B) during   (C) until   (D) while

19. Columbus is the capital of Ohio and _____ largest city.

(A) its   (B) it's   (C) that   (D) that's

20. Her new comic book is _____ more amusing than the previous ones.

(A) much   (B) too   (C) very   (D) well

21. Nothing interesting ever _____ around here.

(A) happens   (B) is happened   (C) happening   (D) are happened

22. I've already _____ allowance this month.

(A) been down on   (B) come down from   (C) gone through with
(D) run out of

23. _____ what to say, she kept silent.

(A) As knowing   (B) Didn't know   (C) Knowing not   (D) Not knowing

24. In old age, I am beginning to _____ my father.

(A) resemble   (B) resemble like   (C) resemble to   (D) resemble with

25. I realized that I _____ my umbrella in his car.

(A) have left   (B) had left   (C) leave   (D) left

26. This type of smartphone _____ well in Japan.

(A) is sold   (B) is being sold   (C) sell   (D) sells

27. You had better not _____ that subject.

(A) discuss   (B) discuss about   (C) to discuss   (D) to discuss about

28. Remember _____ off your computer before leaving today.

(A) to be turned   (B) to turn   (D) turning   (C) to turning

29. Employees _____ in the office after 6 p.m. should inform the security personnel when they leave.

(A) intending stay   (B) stayed   (C) staying   (D) to stay

30. Did you _____ up with an idea for a new product?

(A) become   (B) come   (C) go   (D) take

31. Simon _____ to substitute for Paul in the soccer match.

(A) asked   (B) asks   (C) was asked   (D) will ask

32. He _____ ever studies, except before exams.

(A) does   (B) often   (C) hardly   (D) increasingly

33. I couldn't make _____ understood in English.

(A) it   (B) me   (C) mine   (D) myself

Read the text that follows. A word or phrase is missing in some of the sentences. Select the best answer to complete the text.

Questions 34–36 refer to the following e-mail.

FROM: Manager, General Affairs
TO: All employees
DATE: March 10th, 20___
SUBJECT: Mr. Richard Carpenter's visit

Mr. Richard Carpenter, COO at our partner in the U.S., Stanton Enterprises, will be

visiting Tokyo next month, and will spend a large portion of his time here with us.

We have arranged a series of meetings and other events, detailed below. Please

make yourself ____ the arrangements so that you can participate as appropriate
      34

and show him the proper courtesy during his stay here.

On 3rd, soon after his arrival, we will have an informal reception here in the

offices. This will probably be around 3 p.m. but we will confirm the time on

the day. The reception will be in the main meeting room. Everyone not out on

business should attend. Those engaged in urgent work can just pay a quick visit

to say hello. If he is ____ his flight, we will call a halt after about an hour; otherwise,
      35

the reception may continue for some time.

On 4th, we will have a business meeting in the morning, at around 10 a.m.

We would like all section chiefs ____.
      36

---

34. (A) aware of   (B) beware of   (C) care for   (D) careful of

35. (A) exhausted at   (B) tired from   (C) tired of   (D) weary

36. (A) attend   (B) attending   (C) attention   (D) to attend

READING COMPREHENSION

Read the text that follows. Select the best answer for each question.

Questions 37–40 refer to the following article.

Students and other young people looking for something interesting to do in vacations and a way to gain useful experience—as well as a chance to practice English—should consider a rail trip through Europe, which is made convenient by Eurail Passes.

A Eurail Pass is a special train ticket that can be used in Europe as many times as you like for a certain number of days or weeks. Most students based in Asia used to buy the Select Pass, which was a cost-effective option but required you to choose four neighboring countries in advance, or a Regional Pass. These have been phased out and instead the Global Pass, which allows travel to 33 countries, has been reduced in price. Unless you plan to visit only a single country, in which case a One Country Pass will fit the bill, this is the one you want.

The Eurail Pass itself isn't too expensive, but of course the Pass is not your only expense: you will also need to buy a plane ticket to Europe, and of course you need the money for your accommodations in Europe. To reduce expense, it is best to avoid the summer vacation even though that is the time of year when it is easiest to find the time to go traveling. Flights are much cheaper in the spring vacation, as are accommodations. To further save on accommodations, it is best to look for youth hostels rather than hotels. Another trick is to plan your travels so that you take night trains whenever possible, which also saves you the trouble of finding a place to stay.

---

37. According to the writer of this article, what kind of Eurail Pass is of most interest to students from Asia?

(A) The Global Pass
(B) The Select Pass
(C) The One Country Pass
(D) The Regional Pass

38. What is a Eurail Global Pass?

  (A) A special ticket that allows you to travel by rail in many countries in Europe
  (B) A special ticket that allows you to travel on rail systems throughout the world
  (C) A special ticket that allows you to travel on rail and bus systems
  (D) An alternative name for the Select Pass

39. When is the best time for students to travel in Europe?

  (A) Exam time
  (B) The spring vacation
  (C) The summer vacation
  (D) The winter vacation

40. Which of the following is NOT recommended in the passage as a way to save money?

  (A) Buying a Eurail Pass
  (B) Staying at a youth hostel
  (C) Taking a night train
  (D) Traveling in the summer vacation

テーマ別演習：スキル高める TOEIC® L&R テスト
SHARPENING YOUR TOEIC® L&R TEST SKILLS: STANDARD

検印
省略

©2023 年 1 月 31 日　第 1 版発行

編著者　　　　　　　　安浪　誠祐
　　　　　　　　　　Richard S. Lavin
発行者　　　　　　　　小川　洋一郎
発売所　　　　　　　株式会社朝日出版社
　　　　101-0065　東京都千代田区西神田 3-3-5
　　　　　　　　　　電話（03）3239-0271
　　　　　　　　　　FAX（03）3239-0479
　　　　　　　e-mail: text-e@asahipress.com
　　　　　　　振替口座　00140-2-46008
　　　　組版・Office haru ／製版・錦明印刷

乱丁、落丁本はお取り替えいたします
ISBN 978-4-255-15700-9 C1082